W9-BNI-727

THE
ISRAEL
OMEN II

THE
ISRAEL
OMEN II

The Approaching Cataclysm

DAVID BRENNAN

The Israel Omen II

© 2011 by David Brennan All rights reserved. No part of this book may be reproduced or utilized in any form, or by any electronic, mechanical, or other means, without the prior written permission of the publisher.

Website for this book: www.IsraelOmen.com

ISBN: 978-0-615-52656-0

Retailers and distributors qualify for special discounts on bulk purchases. For more information, email Teknon Publishing at: contact@IsraelOmen.com

To all who are watchful and sober.

With pleasure a special thanks is extended to all that helped with the editing and proofing process. To Susan Meindl for the professional job she did in editing and proofing. And for their laborious efforts in proofing I thank both of my sons, David and Paul as well as my old friend Clarke Kissel.

TABLE OF CONTENTS

PART ONE

Divine Warnings

CHAPTER ONE

The 900-Pound Prophetic Gorillas

After completing *The Israel Omen* in early 2009, and along with it the necessity of being immersed in the ten events that make up the body of that work, it was with great interest that I sat back to observe the actions of the new Obama administration in regard to the Middle East, and Israel in particular. After watching the new administration march month after month into history, the most obvious question continued to present itself: would future events confirm the ten historically severe catastrophes, and their eerie coincidences to efforts at removing the fabled Promised Land from Israel, or would the phenomena suddenly cease, becoming nothing more than an interesting anomaly of Mideast diplomacy? Along with that question a second presented itself in lock-step with the first, like a faithful friend on a common journey: would the "Political-Catastrophe-Matrix" in the final chapter of *The Israel Omen* continue to provide guidance in what to look for in the coming days, a strange roadmap of sorts, to future disasters?

Both questions go beyond a simple academic or even morbid interest in disasters, and in fact strike at the heart of one of the great and raging debates of our time, the debate between faith and science. As knowledge has increased, taking grand steps forward especially in recent years, man has largely begun to place his faith in science, replacing the faith embraced by his forefathers. To those that embrace this new faith, the entire notion that the Bible is a message from the Divine, the Creator of science, is relegated to the category of superstition, a concept whose day has passed. Many believe that science has an answer for every question that man can ask, given enough time. This observation is in no way made to challenge the benefits of science, nor to denigrate the pursuit of such knowledge, but to challenge the notion that science can answer the spiritual questions that appear to be arising, especially in this day that includes a growing number of prophetic fulfillments. Questioning the spiritual side of life has, in a sense, become a prerequisite of most aspiring scientists, if they are to be accepted by their peers. As such, the idea that catastrophes are somehow related to the violation of a Divine promise and the fulfillment of a Divine warning has not only been discarded by science, but science appears impotent to even study it. However, as the number of "coincidences" reviewed within *The Israel Omen* and *The Israel Omen II* continues to mount, the typical secular explanation that "it is all just a coincidence" begins to have an almost humor effect on the listener. Whether or not we have arrived at that place is for you to decide.

* * * * * * *

Since the rebirth of Israel, the world appears to have entered a period of prophetic fulfillment unseen in two thousand years. From the miraculous Jewish victory in their 1948 war for independence to the famed Six-Day War wherein holy Jerusalem was restored to Israeli control, the prophetic pages of the Bible have exploded to life. Now with the world gathering against Israel, ostensibly in an effort toward "peace," here too we see what was foretold in the ancient texts unfolding according to script. These prophetic events, studied and speculated upon by Bible scholars for centuries are occurring during a time when knowledge is greatly increasing and people are traveling extensively-both characteristics unique to the twentieth century and fulfilling prophecy relating to descriptions of the general *times* foretold. In spite of these and a multitude of other ancient prophecies unfolding today, there are *scoffers* at the notion that this is so. But they, too, were prophesized to be present during the *times* as well.

And then there is the much observed gathering of international forces, organizations, powers, and laws that are creating a structure for governance across the border of nations. Such a system, encompassing financial, military, and diplomatic realms is unique in the annals of world history. Yet, this, too, was expected and is breathing life into other old prophetic words. But there is more. With the advent of computers and nuclear weapons more props have appeared on the prophetic stage. The first one, computers, enables the prophesized control over individuals that will eventually come, especially as it relates to commerce. The other appears to fulfill the detailed descriptions of untold destruction we are assured by the ancient words will undoubtedly unfold. As all these props are securely placed on the world stage, so too are increasing earthquakes, the significant kind, as well as a terrible tsunami that has brought great destruction, both signs the Scriptures promised would be present during that *time*. The world stage is set with many of the necessary prophetic props in place, the actors waiting in the wings, ready to begin their roles in a dramatic prophetic event spoken of and studied by Bible scholars for almost two thousand years. But there is a problem, and it is not a small one. There is a 900-pound gorilla on the stage, and it must be removed before the main player, the dreaded world leader can appear.

THE 900-POUND GORILLA

It appears that *The Israel Omen* "coincidences" may, in their own right, represent a piece of a much broader prophetic puzzle, one that appears to be coming together especially as it relates to America. Placed properly, this puzzle piece is allowing new insights to be gleaned as to what might happen next, if these are the *times* warned of. With revolution in the Middle East and great economic upheaval across Europe, the prophetic landscape appears to be well tilled. If the current generation is chosen to live in the much awaited *times,* then there are certain questions that immediately rise to the forefront of one's mind. For those who love America and are familiar with the prophetic script, the most pressing question is why the world's only superpower is so silent during those terrible days. With that question there invariably dances in the back of the mind fear, mixed with incredulousness that this is so. It is especially puzzling since it was America that ultimately defeated the German Kaiser, Adolf Hitler, Japan's Tojo, the Soviet Union, and a host of smaller, but no less dark forces throughout the combative twentieth century. And in spite of the many unfortunate changes in morals over the last several decades, the tendency of America to stand in opposition to despotic leaders is still deeply ingrained in the national psyche. America is so militarily powerful at present that no group of nations would dare attempt to frontally attack her. That, in effect, makes America the proverbial 900-pound gorilla on the prophetic stage, leaving no room for other characters to emerge.

This 900 pound gorilla creates a problem that must be resolved if the *times* foretold are really at hand. The problem is this. The coming world leader will also be a 900-pound gorilla, and for him to enter the prophetic stage the American gorilla must first depart. Both simply cannot fit. Based on what is foretold in the ancient words that this world leader will do, America simply would not stand for it, regardless of who the president is.

If these are, indeed, the *times* that the prophets wrote about and Biblical scholars have speculated on over the centuries, then events are about to unfold that will shock even the most resilient observer. Part of the shock must include an altering in the current world power order that America and her true friends will find appalling. Even under President Obama whose ideology apparently requires a dismantling, of sorts, of U.S. alliances and leadership, that effort is painfully inadequate to accomplish the task of removing America as the dominant world force, allowing room on the prophetic world stage for the promised world leader to appear. In spite of the nature of the Obama Administration and especially its foreign policy, it is incapable of truly altering the fact of American power. But except for those nations that have entered the orbit of radical Islam, even those countries most offended by Obama's actions have no other option than turning to America when the chips are down. And as it pertains to China, in spite of that nation's real strides of industrialization, it is no match against American power into the foreseeable future. Simply stated, as long as American power is even remotely what it is today, the *times* foretold cannot proceed. Some students of the Bible engage in the greatest theoretical gyrations to clear the world stage for the coming, dreaded world leader, but the extent of their efforts only reinforce the above logic.

In the Second World War, after Pearl Harbor, there was some hesitancy within the ranks of the Third Reich in declaring war against America. Ultimately, its pact with Japan won the debate, but its leadership was not pleased with the prospect of facing the industrial might of the United States. Hitler, as a form of character the likes of which the coming world leader will be, would have not dared launch his war in Europe had America been as militarily aggressive and powerful as what she currently is.

But there is the rub. If these are the *times,* then something is needed in the future to kick off the more ugly side of things, in a rather shocking way. Because if these are the *times,* then for them to proceed according to script the current world power structure must be replaced with one of a much more fierce nature.

An answer to that question may now have begun to arise from the developing strategic/prophetic picture. The answer arises from what appear to be emphatic Divine warnings that have been given for two decades to America and the world, as documented within *The Israel Omen* and now *The Israel Omen II*. Those warnings, combined with current political and strategic realities may be pointing to what starts the truly terrible events promised to characterize that *time*. But, along with those warnings, there has appeared a most disturbing threat against America, and it is one that remains almost unspoken. That development is discussed in Part Two, The Unspoken Threat to America.

ANOTHER 900-POUND GORILLA

From the prophet Daniel we know that the dastardly, coming world leader will eventually *confirm* a *covenant* relating to Israel *with many for seven years*. We also know that he will sit in the rebuilt Jewish temple, an apparent replica of the one old King Solomon had built, and declare himself a god, representing a moment of great insult to the true God. Yet, rebuilding that temple is another 900-pound prophetic gorilla that must be dealt with. The temple must be rebuilt and by the Jews, but here is the problem. It must be rebuilt on the Temple Mount. Currently any such Jewish attempt to do so would bring worldwide Muslim rage and immediate war. To put that in proper perspective, consider this. So severe were Jewish concerns relating to Muslim religious sensitivities that, after Israel captured the Mount in the 1967 Six-Day War, they immediately turned it over to Muslim religious authorities to oversee. To put that in proper context, this took place after Israeli forces routed the Arab armies surrounding her, leaving no immediate enemy to prevent any action the Jewish government might have taken relating to the Mount. But Israel, understanding the extreme nature of Muslim sensitivities, knew how to handle the issue.

There is presently much speculation that a possible treaty between Israel and the Arabs, bringing a "peace" between them that will include a provision that allows the Jews to rebuild their holy temple. But that is rubbish. The current political reality in the Middle East makes such a concession in any agreement an absolute impossibility. Simply stated, the Arabs would currently be willing to die by the millions to prevent such Jewish actions at their holy site and will not negotiate it into any treaty. Any Arab leader that hinted at such a thing would probably lose his followers. If, as so many within Christian prophetic circles today proclaim, these are the *times* that were foretold, then the current Scriptural and strategic realities are in dramatic conflict making it impossible for the temple to be rebuilt in the immediate future. Therefore, a way must be found if these are the *times* warned of.

There is simply no getting around it as two factors must occur if the much anticipated *times* have finally arrived. First, America must recede as a superpower, allowing the promised world leader to rise. Second, someone must convince the Arabs to allow the Jews to rebuild their Holy Temple on the Temple Mount, grounds Muslims around the world consider holy as well. Simply stated, for both of these events to take place, it is necessary for a radical shift in the worldwide matrix of power to occur, and that is where the warnings considered in *The Israel Omen,* combined with strategic developments bring into focus the most likely answer to the most significant question...what is next?

The Israel Omen II will present the case that a world-shaking event, terrible enough to alter the present world power matrix is, quite possibly, approaching and that this is really what *The Israel Omen* warnings have been all about. The approaching event would most likely mark the beginning of the much warned of *times.* There is even some evidence that the approaching cataclysm will be a faint foreshadowing of another much more significant prophetic event expected to occur sometime down the road during the *times*. For those of you that have not read *The Israel Omen*, the following chapter will bring you up to speed with a brief synopsis of the ten historical events covered therein. Also, it will cover Zechariah's *four horns* prophecy, an old prophecy that appears to have begun unfolding in 2003. However, because of the significance of the Zechariah *four horns* discovery, a broader justification that this prophecy is unfolding will be presented herein than is found within *The Israel Omen*.

Thereafter, we will look at the Biblical basis for the "coincidence" of disasters associated with efforts to remove the Promised Land from Israel. Then we will look at what "coincidences" have occurred since *The Israel Omen* was completed.

CHAPTER TWO

The Israel Omen Warnings

The main motivation in writing *The Israel Omen* centered on the discovery that an amazing series of "coincidences" had taken place since 1991. Those "coincidences" involved the fact that each time a serious diplomatic effort to remove the Biblical "Promised Land" from Israel *advanced*, a *historically* severe catastrophe would occur. In most cases the catastrophes took place to the very day that the diplomatic effort began. Significantly, none of the catastrophes were your run-of-the-mill type, all being of a *historical* nature. Interestingly, each of the diplomatic efforts toward the removal of this Biblical Promised Land shared the fact that they were either a *new effort*, or an established effort that suddenly made *progress*. In other words, they represented an *advance* toward removing the land from Israeli control. In the case of an already established effort where diplomats gathered but made no progress, nothing of a historical nature appeared to take place "coincidentally" with that effort. A good example of this phenomena would be the series of diplomatic gatherings christened the Madrid Peace Conferences that met between the years 1991 and 1993. After the initial breakthrough "peace" conference in 1991, which saw the "Perfect Storm" strike on the day the conference opened, the next two conferences experienced no historical catastrophe associated with them. But neither of those conferences made progress toward removing the fabled Promised Land from the Jews.

Interestingly, and we will look at the potential significance of this later, all of the efforts to remove the Promised Land from Israel since 1991 shared the same theme, they would bring about a long awaited era of "peace" for the most troubled region of the world. Notably, that region happens to be the one that the entire world has a great stake in experiencing "peace" in since becoming completely dependent on the oil produced there. This has caused the eyes of the entire world to turn inexorably to the Middle East, much more so than any other region of the world. From a strategic standpoint, the region is the most important on the globe. Any war there represents a potential threat to the flow of oil, which strikes at the heart of the well-being of the nations of the world. As a result all nations have developed a great interest in seeing "peace" finally take place between Israel and the Palestinians, believing that such a "peace" is critical. So important is the Middle East and the perception that a "peace" must be secured there, that various presidents and prime ministers have attempted to pull the mythical "Excalibur" of Middle East "peace" from the stone of intransigence, only to fail and then suffer a reduction in stature. And since none have been worthy of the effort, the one that does make "peace" will gain greatly, worthy of Excalibur and destined for history. But the Excalibur of Middle East "peace" remains embedded in stone, only to be gazed upon longingly by those that would be great.

Adding to that strange litany of catastrophe "coincidences" catalogued in *The Israel Omen* was another discovery, one involving a modern political group that appears to have risen out of the pages of the Bible. The discovery involved the international group officially referred to as the Quartet. As a creation of President George W. Bush, the goal of this group is to bring "peace" to the Israelis and Palestinians by removing large tracts of land from Israel and giving them to create a new nation called Palestine. Since no one leader could pull Excalibur from the rock, now four have united to try. However, this group appears to have been specifically warned of by the old prophet Zechariah with their actions since 2003 unfolding according to the Biblical narrative. This discovery constitutes one of the warnings that appear to be accumulating in our midst.

For those who have read *The Israel Omen,* what is contained within this chapter will represent a very brief rendition of chapters four through fourteen, the "coincidences" of catastrophes relative to the diplomatic efforts to remove the "Promised Land" from Israel. With so many historically notable catastrophes lining up against the backdrop of "peace" efforts, it is possible a much more significant Biblical warning is unfolding. If this is true, then the impending event may not only be catastrophic, but cataclysmic.

WARNINGS SINCE 1991 ASSOCIATED WITH EFFORTS TO REMOVE THE PROMISED LAND FROM ISRAEL

COINCIDENCE NUMBER ONE

In October 1991, after months of intense efforts, James Baker, Secretary of State for the Bush administration, succeeded in pulling together for the first time a gathering of Israel and her Muslim enemies for the purpose of talking "peace." The Madrid Peace Conference, named after the capital of Spain where it would be held, was a breakthrough for those working toward a Middle East peace agreement, bringing together the warring parties for talks. Of course, the main effort toward "peace" involved the removal of vast tracts of land from Israel, land promised them in the ancient Holy Scriptures. The conference began its efforts on October 30, with delegates issuing their opening statements. But as the conference was launched, something else on the other side of the Atlantic Ocean was also beginning.

A storm, referred to as "The Perfect Storm," began striking a bewildered New England coast. The residents along the coast were surprised because the storm was unexpected, so much so that meteorologists christened it a "once in a hundred year" storm. It was what occurred days earlier that made it so unique. On October 28 and well into the Atlantic Ocean, three storm systems converged into one mighty storm, causing weather experts to call it a "freak of nature." However, as unusual as it is for three storm systems to converge into one, what the combined system did next was what put it into the history books.

After converging, and still in the Atlantic and posing no threat to the United States, the storm suddenly reversed course and begin moving west instead of on the normal eastern path. With this strange reversal, it headed directly for the unprepared New England coast. That rare reversal is called "retrogression" and added to the "Perfect Storm's" mystery of how it was created. On October 30, 1991, just as the Madrid Peace Conference began meeting on the other side of the ocean, the Perfect Storm began striking the coast. And along with the storm came incredible one-hundred foot waves, ultimately leading to a Hollywood movie. Was the storm's timing just a coincidence? It would easily be considered so if the story of coincidences stopped here. But, the story does not end here with the Perfect Storm, it only begins.

COINCIDENCE NUMBER TWO

At the conclusion of the Madrid Peace Conference, an agreement was reached from both Israel and the Palestinians that they would continue to meet under the Madrid banner of negotiations. Those meetings would take place in Washington D.C., but would ultimately produce no progress. The main obstacle to "progress" was the prime minister of Israel himself, Yitzhak Shamir. Shamir did not believe that trading land for peace would work and feared the security risk for Israel was too great. However, when Shamir lost the next election to Yitzhak Rabin, everything changed.

Rabin believed that trading land to Israel's enemies would placate them, bringing a much desired peace. With the agreeable Rabin replacing the intransigent Shamir, the Bush administration could not have been happier, believing that finally "progress" could be made toward a Middle East peace that had eluded presidents since Harry Truman. Now, unlike the previous Madrid Conferences, "progress" would begin to be made.

On August 24, 1992, the next round of the Madrid Peace Conference began. Unlike the previous rounds, this one was destined to be very different. A spokeswoman for the Syrian government that participated in the negotiations would reminisce weeks later of the difference in the new Israeli attitude, noting how much more accommodating it was compared to the previous Shamir government. She noted a "different style" existed in the Israeli delegation with Israeli statements representing a change from the prior government's positions. The most striking difference was that they acknowledged the principal of "land for peace." However, as the "peace" conference was opening in Washington D.C., the President's attention was drawn to southern Florida to a calamity that had taken place only hours earlier in the dead of night on August 24, 1992.

Hurricane Andrew, the most destructive storm in U.S. history, at that time, had slammed into the south Florida coast. As a feared category five storm on the Saffir-Simpson Scale, it had sustained winds of 160-165 mph with gusts to 200 mph! Andrew would rank fourth in all-time severity behind three storms infamous in their own day: the 1935 hurricane that hit the Florida Keys, 1969's Camille, and of more recent notoriety, 2005's Katrina.

Historically severe, Hurricane Andrew became the second "coincidence" relative to efforts to remove the land from Israel, promised her in the ancient Hebrew Scriptures. However, with Rabin still in power, Israel was ready to take the next step in the United States' effort of "land for peace."

COINCIDENCE NUMBER THREE

After the Madrid Peace Conference in which Rabin had been so accommodating, it would not take long for the next "peace" effort to take place. So significant was the progress at his first conference that both sides were able to move forward on a host of issues. With critics of the efforts on both sides, Israeli and Palestinian leaders decided to have representatives meet in Oslo, Norway in secret. Here, with no prying eyes, their representatives could iron out a multitude of issues. To further cover the ploy, representatives of both sides continued to meet in Washington under the Madrid Peace Conference banner. For Israel the choice was clear. The United States, its most important friend in the world and the only superpower, was pressing hard for the tiny Jewish nation to give land to its enemy in the name of "peace." So important was the United States to Israel, that any thought of alienating that relationship was not an option.

The secret negotiations began in April 1993, and reached a successful conclusion in August of that year. With a representative of the willing Rabin at the negotiating table, the result was a breakthrough agreement giving the Palestinians control over large stretches of Judea and Samaria, the ancient lands of Israel known as the Promised Land. On September 13, 1993, a month after the successful negotiations ended, a ceremony was held on the South Lawn of the White House. Before representatives of over 100 countries and 3000 onlookers, Israeli Prime Minister Yitzhak Rabin and Palestinian leader Yasser Arafat signed the historical agreement, much to the amazement of the world.

In April 1993, just as negotiations to remove Israeli control over the fabled Promised Land began, a weather event believed by some not to have happened in five hundred years also started. A weather system referred to as the Bermuda High, which usually sits over the Atlantic Ocean at that time of the year, moved farther north and west than was the norm, the result being the creation of a dam of air that stopped Midwest storms dead in their tracts, not allowing them to move off to the East Coast to deposit the bulk of their showers in the Atlantic. The end result of this highly unusual atmospheric circumstance would be a deluge of almost Biblical proportions.

The flooding that resulted and lasted from April until August of 1993, produced what the National Weather Service would declare "one of the most significant and damaging natural disasters ever to hit the United States." They pointed out that "the flood was unusual in the magnitude of the crests, the number of record crests, the large area impacted, and the length of time the flood was an issue."

The Great Flood of 1993, as it would later be called, was fed by rainfall, which produced flooding that exceeded 500-year recurrence intervals. In plain English, it was a very, very rare natural disaster. In total, 92 locations set record crests during the Great Flood of 1993. The final price tag would hit $15 billion, making it one of the most expensive natural disasters in U.S. history.

With the best of intentions, U.S. Middle East policy had become one of bartering the "Promised Land" in return for a promised peace. As Israel's best friend in the world, and the only superpower, the U.S. was in a unique position to pressure the Jews into concessions, and it did so. The fruit of those efforts and secret negotiations from April to August 1993, resulted in a peace accord whose ultimate goal was the removal of Israeli control over the ancient lands of Judea and Samaria. Unwittingly, U.S. Middle East policy had again challenged a direct promise of God, according to the ancient writings. Alongside that challenge, however, "one of the most significant and damaging natural disasters ever to hit the United States" unfolded from April to August, month by month, coinciding with the negotiations.

COINCIDENCE NUMBER FOUR

Having rebuffed the Israeli overtures immediately after the Six-Day War to return the captured land for true peace, Syria was now having second thoughts. In 1993 after seeing the Palestinians make "progress" toward some form of resolution of their issue with the Jews, Syrian leader Assad began making overtures toward Washington, indicating that "peace" with Israel was now possible. As a result, the Clinton Administration decided to test the waters with the Syrian leader to see just how serious he was. In a meeting on January 16, 1994 in Geneva, Switzerland, Clinton would find out.

In a five-hour meeting between Assad and Clinton, the Syrian leader stated he would establish normal diplomatic relations with Israel in exchange for the return of the land captured in the Six-Day War. Adding,

If the leaders of Israel have sufficient courage to respond, a new era of security and stability in which there will be normal peaceful relations among all shall dawn.

Two days after the Clinton–Assad meeting, Israeli Prime Minister Rabin issued a statement warning his fellow Israelis that they should be ready to pay "a painful price" for peace. The price tag would be the return of the strategically significant Golan Heights, a buffer of protection against further attacks from its northern enemy. Clinton had obviously spoken to Rabin the day before his announcement, encouraging him to make the deal by placing more of the Promised Land on the auction block with another enemy that had previously tried to destroy the country. It is apparent from the timing of the Clinton-Assad meeting and the Rabin announcement that Clinton had spoken to Rabin on January 17, the day after Clinton's meeting with Assad and the day before Rabin's statement.

On the very day Clinton was pressuring the accommodating Rabin for Israel to give back more of the ancient Promised Land, the Northridge Earthquake struck California, killing 57 people and causing over $25 billion in damages, the second most costly natural disaster in U.S. history at that time. The Northridge Earthquake was the highest instrumentally recorded earthquake in an urban area in North American history.

COINCIDENCE NUMBER FIVE

On June 5, 2001, President George W. Bush suddenly decided to involve his new administration in an effort to settle the Middle East conflict. It was announced on that day that CIA Director George Tenet would go to the region in an attempt to get the recommendations of the "Mitchell Report" implemented. The "Mitchell Report" detailed the issues in the conflict and recommended solutions. If enacted, Israel would lose more control over the ancient Promised Land, all due to pressure from the new administration. As the announcement was being made in Washington to send the CIA Director to the region, something strange began taking place in the Gulf of Mexico.

Weathermen in the president's home state of Texas had been watching a tropical disturbance located about 150 miles offshore in the northwestern Gulf for several days. However, the system "wasn't given much chance of strengthening," according to the *Houston Chronicle*. But by 2 p.m., about the time at which the White House was announcing the Tenet trip to the Middle East, a Hurricane Hunter aircraft keeping track of developments in the Gulf reported that the system had suddenly developed into a full-blown tropical storm just off the coast of Texas. According to an official at the National Weather Service, "the storm developed so rapidly there was no time to react."

In referring to what was now a mystery storm just off the Texas coast, Charles Roeseler, a forecaster at the National Weather Service, observed that "it went right from nothing to a tropical storm." The Houston Chronicle would later report "the storm had not even been a blip on the forecasters' radar screens twelve hours earlier, before it became the first named storm of the season." Tropical Storm Allison, as it would be named, would be considered by meteorologists to be the "nation's worst tropical storm" ever and unanimously "decreed by weather experts as a deluge of historic proportions for its rainfall totals, flooding and widespread effect." All of this on the day the new Bush Administration announced its intention to become actively engaged against the land of Israel.

COINCIDENCE NUMBER SIX

Not long after the administration of President George W. Bush took power in Washington, the new president gained the unfortunate reputation within Saudi Arabian ruling circles as being a lightweight on matters of peace in the Middle East. So ingrained had this belief become, that on August 9, 2001, the Saudi Ambassador to Great Britain, Ghazi Qussaibi, was quoted in a London-based Arabic newspaper as saying that "Bush knows very little, and is ruled by complexes, the most important is to avoid looking like his predecessor and his father." The ambassador then went on to say that in the short time the new president had been in office, he had already succeeded in making enemies out of America's friends.

In a series of articles in February 2002, *Washington Post* staff writers Robert Kaiser and David Ottaway revealed that, in August 2001, Saudi ruler Crown Prince Abdullah sent a strongly worded letter to President Bush, admonishing him for what the Saudi leader saw as his one-sided approach to the Israeli-Palestinian conflict. But the letter represented much more than a simple admonishment, and in fact was a notice ending the alliance between the two countries that had begun under Roosevelt, and had been nurtured by presidents ever since. The letter sent the Bush

White House into a tailspin, causing it to launch a frantic effort to repair the critical relationship.

What Bush would offer the desert kingdom in his effort to repair the relationship would shock the Saudis as much as their staggering letter had impacted the White House. As reported by Kaiser and Ottaway, Bush's response was given in a letter to the Saudi Ambassador within 36 hours of having received the Saudi letter. Within it, Bush committed the United States to a new Middle East policy and one none of his predecessors had ever gone so far as to offer. The president stated:

> I firmly believe the Palestinian people have a right to self-determination and to live peacefully and securely in their own state, in their own homeland, just as the Israelis have the right to live peacefully and safely in their own state.

Based on the Bush letter, the United States would, for the first time, support the establishment of a Palestinian state on the land promised to Israel in the ancient Hebrew Scriptures. Essentially, U.S. policy was now supporting the permanent removal of the land from Israel, effectively reversing the promise of God to the Jews. So surprised was Prince Abdullah and the ruling Saudi family that they began showing the letter to various Arab leaders, essentially bragging about what amounted to a significant breakthrough in favor of the Palestinians. However, to make certain that the Bush Administration was serious they asked for the new policy to be announced as soon as possible by the White House.

The Bush Administration agreed to the Saudis request and over the weekend of September 8 and 9 officials from both countries began planning what would happen next. The approach decided upon was for a Bush speech, and possibly one from Secretary of State Colin Powell where both would officially call for the establishment of a Palestinian state. According to Carl Woodward, in his book *State of Denial*, Bush agreed to publicly come out for a Palestinian state in a "big rollout" planned for the week of September 10, 2001.

COINCIDENCE NUMBER SEVEN & EIGHT

(NOTE: Relates to *Zechariah's "Four Horns"* to be discussed later)

Following the attacks of September 11, and now consumed with the "war on terror," the Bush Administration placed the Israeli-Palestinian dispute on the back burner for the balance of 2001 and throughout all of 2002. But, by 2003, Bush was ready to fulfill his promise to the Saudi Crown Prince, and began his push for the creation of a Palestinian state in the middle of the Promised Land. The approach he would take appears to have begun a prophetic clock, bringing to life an ancient prophetic warning given by the prophet Zechariah. The prophecy given some 2500 years ago warned that a group of four political powers would unite sometime in the future with the goal of *scattering* the land of Israel.

In cooperation with Russia, the European Union and United Nations, the United States created the "road map" to peace process. Within this new "peace" effort, the newly constituted group of four political powers would follow the U.S. script that the only way to peace in the Middle East was for Israel to relinquish large tracts of the Promised Land in return for promises of peace. With great anticipation, the newly formed Quartet, as it would be called, met on April 30, 2003. At 10:30 a.m., President Bush summed-up the Quartet's position on the dispute:

> The government of Israel, as the terror threat is removed and
> security improves, must take steps to support the emergence of
> a viable and credible Palestinian state...

As the new and grand gathering to remove the Promised Land from Israel was being kicked off, something else was also just beginning in the midsection of the U.S. In over a dozen states across the region, tornados began a rampage that would continue for over three weeks. Before it was over 562 tornados would strike in what weather experts would call "the worst weather in U.S. history." It all began on April 30, 2003, the day the Quartet met.

Just as the "worst weather in U.S. history" was ending, the European continent, home to another major player of the Quartet, began to experience something not seen in at least two hundred fifty years. A heat wave of historical and staggering proportions began striking. After the heat wave finally ended three months later, the extent of the catastrophe began to be revealed. Some estimates indicated that the tragic death toll reached as high as 52,000! That made it one of the worst climate-related disasters in recorded Western history.

COINCIDENCE NUMBER NINE

In February 2001, the hawkish Israeli lawmaker Ariel Sharon was elected Prime Minister of his country. During his colorful career he had worked his way up to the rank of Major General within the Israeli Defense Forces and in the 1970s was known for his feisty attitude, sometimes even disobeying orders from his superiors. He had experienced occasional setbacks, such as when a commission report found him indirectly responsible for a massacre of Palestinians by Lebanese Christian militiamen. But as an enthusiastic supporter of the movement to settle the West Bank with Israelis, his career eventually resurrected, resulting eventually in his assuming the top Israeli post in 2001. Taking office just one month after the Republican George W. Bush went to Washington, it was expected the two would have an unspoken understanding of the security needs of Israel. From common political reports on the two, it was also expected that both would see eye-to-eye on the "peace" process. But sometimes perceptions can be deceiving.

Occasionally, those we think we know the best surprise us the most. And so it was with Ariel Sharon. Perhaps they were too close, Sharon able to be swayed from the more rational side of his mind by his friend the President. Whatever the reason, by 2005, Bush was able to convince

Sharon to abandon Gaza, dismantling settlements there and withdrawing all Israeli forces from the area and, in the process, shocking his supporters and surprising the world. Now, because of Sharon, the restored ancient land of Sampson and Delilah was once again outside of Israeli control. On August 23, 2005, the Israeli Foreign Office would officially declare the painful Jewish removal from Gaza complete. However, what continued were the deep feelings of betrayal felt by those removed from the land they were assured by the ancient Hebrew Scriptures was theirs.

After the Israeli withdrawal from Gaza was completed, the Palestinians in the area chose to use their new independence to attack Israel with massive rocket barrages on a regular basis, instead of focusing on building the nation they had been protesting to obtain. Along with the increase in rocket attacks would come the increased realization among Israelis that swapping land for peace did not work. But those results did not appear to impact the perception of world leaders who continued to believe in it.

However, on August 23, 2005, the same day that Israeli officials declared the removal of the Jews from Gaza complete, something else on the other side of the world was just beginning. In the Atlantic Ocean near the Bahamas, tropical depression number twelve was noticed by the National Weather Service for the first time. The next day it strengthened to a tropical storm and was named Katrina. The rest of the story, as we know, is now history.

COINCIDENCE NUMBER TEN

(NOTE: Relates to *Zechariah's "Four Horns"*)

With the "progress" of the 2005 Israeli withdrawal from Gaza, President Bush sought to add to that "success" by restarting the stalled "road map" process involving the Quartet. Since the initial Quartet effort that began April 30, 2003, the process had become dormant. But Bush was able to convince his good friend and former British Prime Minister Tony Blair to assume the position of envoy for the group. Now, with so prominent a person heading up the prophesized group of four, progress would be made.

Blair's efforts would start on July 23, 2007, with his first trip as Quartet envoy to the Middle East. On this maiden voyage to the troubled region he would begin a process that would eventually lead to what would be called the Annapolis Conference. Attended by over 45 nations and international organizations, the conference was held in November of that year.

For the first time in history, the effort to forge a Middle East peace agreement had gone global. The November conference represented a success because it established a framework within which the conflicted parties would work toward resolving the various issues. In fact, the conference became a Promised Land bazaar with the land promised in the ancient Hebrew Scriptures to be exchanged for promises of peace. In its aftermath, the conference was considered a success toward the eventual removal of the ancient lands from Israel, with significant progress having been made. And it all began on July 23, 2007, with the new Quartet envoy, Tony Blair's, visit to the region to gather the parties together for the conference.

However, also during the week of July 23, 2007, an event in the global banking system began unfolding. The lifeblood of the international banking system is liquidity, available cash on hand for banks to meet their legal obligations to depositors. Since available funds within banks vary from day to day, based on withdrawals versus deposits, a bank will often have a surplus of liquidity available for lending in the overnight interbank lending system, where banks lend to other banks. On the other hand, when depositor withdrawals and other immediate obligations exceed available cash, that same bank will enter the interbank lending system to borrow the necessary funds. As with all lending activities, the creditworthiness of the bank is the key factor in determining its participation in these interbank lending transactions and determines what the premium charged for its overnight lending will be. Fear about a bank's creditworthiness would not only result in depositors withdrawing funds but also in that bank's inability to tap the interbank lending system. This inability to accomplish short-term borrowing would create an even more unstable bank and one that would be unlikely to survive as access to funds was cut off.

There is, however, a method of measuring how banks view the risk of lending to each other on a system-wide international banking basis. It is called the Libor-OIS spread. To sum it up, this spread represents the premium charged by banks to lend short-term, uncollateralized funds to other banks overnight. Like an auto insurance policy, the greater the perceived risk, the higher the premium charged. This premium charged by banks to banks is measured in hundredths of one percent and has averaged, between 2001 and July 2007, between 6/100ths and 8/100ths of one percent. Essentially, the small premium indicated that within the international banking community, there was very little concern about the solvency of banks participating in this interbank lending system. That was, however, until July 2007.

The same week the new Quartet envoy, Tony Blair, began his maiden voyage to the Middle East to gather support in an effort to remove the Promised Land from Israel, the international banking system began to break down. On July 26, three days after Blair's trip began, the risk premium jumped 50% to 13/100ths of one percent. Had that been a simple one day anomaly, it would not have been significant. However, the increase of July 26 would mark a historical rise in the premium with it ultimately reaching a staggering 364/100ths, bringing the world financial system to the brink of systemic collapse.

How unlikely was it that the premium charged by banks to banks skyrocketed to such levels? In answer to that question consider this. The probability of certain financial events happening over the course of time can be measured statistically as a sigma event. The higher the sigma number, the less chance of the event occurring. The chance of the premium paid by banks to one another skyrocketing upward as it did was measured as a sigma 6.2 event. Translated into English, that is to say it would take 6,800 years to see such an event take place! Yet, that rare event began the week Tony Blair began his trip to the Middle East to gather the world against the Promised Land.

It is important to note that one through nine of the "coincidences" were first discovered by John McTernan and William Koenig. As indicated, two of the "coincidences" were designated as being related to the *four horns* warned of by the prophet Zechariah.

THE "FOUR HORNS" OF ZECHARIAH

Sometime around 520 B.C., a Hebrew prophet named Zechariah recorded receiving visions from God that revealed the future of mankind. One prophecy by the ancient prophet describes a time in the future when actions will be taken by a group of *four horns*, which Biblically refers to political powers, to remove part of the "Promised Land" from Israel. However, this prophecy warns that those engaged in the effort will experience Divine retribution as a result. Eerily, the prophecy appears to describe the efforts by the current international group called the Quartet. From the King James Bible:

> *Then I lifted up mine eyes and saw, and behold four horns. And I said unto the angel that talked with me, What be these? And he answered me, These are the horns which have scattered Judah, Israel and Jerusalem.* (Zechariah 1:18-19)

In Biblical terms, a *horn* represents political power. The Quartet is comprised of four distinct governmental entities, the United States, Russia, the European Union, and the United Nations. This group has joined together against the lands of Israel, Judah, and Jerusalem with significant gatherings aimed at removal of these lands in the name of "peace."

As we saw earlier in this chapter, the effort on the part of the Quartet (*four horns*) began in earnest on April 30, 2003, with their first gathering as a group dedicated to finding an agreement between the parties in the name of peace. However, any agreement would involve scattering large tracts of the restored Promised Land from the Israelis representing something that the ancient Scriptures indicate would reverse a promise of God. In line with the Biblical warning, April 30, 2003, also marked the beginning of what weather experts at the time described as "the worst weather in U.S. history." It was then immediately followed by the worst heat wave in the last two hundred fifty years in Europe, the other main player in that Quartet effort. After that initial gathering, the next Quartet conference would take place in Annapolis, Maryland at the U.S. Naval Academy in November 2007, and this effort would produce several significant breakthroughs. The effort to pull together that conference was initiated by the new Quartet envoy, the well respected former British Prime Minister, Tony Blair, on July 23, 2007. That date marked the exact week the global financial system began an unraveling that would ultimately lead it to the brink of a systemic collapse, the first since the Great Depression. To continue the words of Zechariah...

And the Lord shewed me four carpenters. Then said I, What come these to do? And he spake, saying, These are the horns which have scattered Judah, so that no man did lift up his head: but these are come to fray them, to cast out the horns of the Gentiles, which lifted up their horn over the land of Judah to scatter it. (Zechariah 1:20-21)

There is much to ponder on what is covered in the above Scriptures, especially as it relates to events that are unfolding against the Promised Land in our day. The first and most obvious is that the Quartet represents a group of *four horns*, political powers that have united against the land, just as Zechariah prophesized would come to pass one day. But, their effort will bring a Divine response with the prophetic *carpenters* coming to *fray them*, or as the word is defined, do battle against.

Some say that this passage in Zechariah of *four horns* represents nations in Israel's distant past which, one by one, and over the course of time, went against the land. However, many Biblical scholars had to take that position because they embraced "replacement" theology, which states that the church replaced Israel Biblically. Therefore, since they were unable to envision Israel actually becoming a nation again, they had to take this position to explain the *four horns* prophecy. But, in 1948, Israel did reappear as a nation, again, against incredible odds. Additionally, the passage itself tells us that it will be a uniting of four political entities at the same time, and not separately. Consider this in the text.

> *Then I lifted up mine eyes and saw, and behold four* **horns***. (PLURAL) And I said unto the angel that talked with me, What be these? And he answered me, These are the* **horns** *(PLURAL) which have scattered Judah, Israel and Jerusalem. And the Lord shewed me four carpenters. Then said I, What come these to do? And he spake, saying, These are the* **horns** *(PLURAL) which have scattered Judah, so that no man did lift up his head: but these are come to fray them, to cast out the* **horns** *(PLURAL) of the Gentiles, which lifted up their* **horn***(SINGULAR) over the land of Judah to scatter it.* (Zechariah 1:18-21, emphasis added)

The text begins and continues to refer to, the *horns* in the plural sense throughout the passage, indicating four separate political entities are at work here. Then, in the last reference, it refers to them in the singular, *horn*, indicating they will act as one, united against the land. In other words, they are *four horns* that ultimately act as a single *horn*. It is only today's Quartet that fills that description. Another approach to this passage states that Zechariah does not specifically name the *four horns* because the readers in his day would simply know who he was talking about since it was referring to nations in Israel's past. But here, too, that analysis is easily refuted. Throughout the Book of Zechariah, the prophet does, in fact, name at least 30 different nations, cities, or regions specifically. He practices throughout his writings the tendency to specifically name political powers but not in the passage in question. The more logical reason that he would have singled out this passage for not having specified the political entities involved, is that he couldn't because several of the *horns* did not yet exist.

But perhaps the most powerful evidence that the modern day Quartet represents the *four horns* spoken of by the prophet is the fact that historically severe catastrophes have occurred with uncanny timing associated with their diplomatic efforts to remove the Promised Land, exactly what the ancient words warned against.

★ ★ ★ ★ ★ ★ ★

Since the Global Financial Crisis that came to a head in the latter half of 2008, and which represented the tenth event covered in *The Israel Omen*, more such "coincidences" have taken place. In the following pages, there are three more such events whose timing is also uncanny to *advances* against the Promised Land: all are historical in their nature. The real development, however, related to events since Barack Obama became U.S. president. Since assuming office, he has engaged in a series of actions relating to the Middle East, and Israel in particular, that were initially puzzling, leaving his opponents as well as his supporters wondering if he was up to the task of dealing with the complex issues in that part of the world. But in his May 19, 2011 speech, where he essentially took the Palestinian position against Israel, making it U.S. policy, the puzzle appears to be getting resolved, the hidden picture forming for all to see. Before we look at the events that have occurred since 2008, it is first necessary to consider why attempting to remove the land from Israel is so dangerous. In other words, what is the basis for the "coincidence" of catastrophes against the efforts to remove the land from Israel? This knowledge is critical in understanding what might be coming next.

CHAPTER THREE

A Divine Oath

I n order to appreciate why such "coincidences" of catastrophes relative to efforts to remove the land from Israel might be taking place, one must go to the ancient Hebrew texts. Deep within pages that were written many centuries ago, a story unfolds centered on the Jewish people of ancient times becoming the focal point of God's attention. It is a story of a relationship between the Jews and their God, one that began when a Jew named Abraham exhibited such great faith in the true God that he was, henceforth, viewed by Him as a friend. Because of Abraham's great faith, God made certain oaths pertaining to him and his descendents.

Much later those descendents of Abraham experienced a terrible famine in the land where they dwelled, forcing them to flee to Egypt, which was a land of plenty in the midst of the great famine. However, after several generations and a great multiplication of their numbers, these descendents became slaves in Egypt, experiencing a very hard life. But their God remembered the promise He had made to Abraham, and delivered His people from the harsh hand of Pharaoh. The Divine method used to accomplish this deliverance is, strangely, of interest to us here today. After promising the descendents of Abraham a land of their own, called Canaan, the Jews demanded that Pharaoh release them from their servitude so that they might go to the land promised them by their God. Eventually, Pharaoh relented but only after experiencing a series of horrific plagues.

The punishing plagues from God against the Egyptians represent some of the most strange and unusual events recorded in the Bible, bringing catastrophe after catastrophe against the powerful Egyptians. Finally, after the last plague, the death of Egypt's first-born children, Pharaoh gave in and allowed the Jews to leave so they could go to the land promised by God. All of this was done so that the Jews could go to this Promised Land. Here are some quotes within the Bible making it clear how important the land God promised the Jews is to Him, speaking an oath of the land to the Jews and their descendents.

In the Book of Exodus, Moses talks about the land promised the Jews, his words spoken just after their release from Egypt:

> *⁵And it shall be when the LORD shall bring thee into the land of the Canaanites, and the Hittites, and the Amorites, and the Hivites, and the Jebusites, which he sware unto thy fathers to give thee, a land flowing with milk and honey, that thou shalt keep this service in this month.* (Exodus 13:5)

After the Israelites, newly freed from Egypt, became unfaithful toward God, Moses implores Him toward mercy. The following passage from Exodus also reiterates Gods oath of the land for the Jews:

> *¹³Remember Abraham, Isaac, and Israel, thy servants, to whom thou swarest by thine own self, and saidst unto them, I will multiply your seed as the stars of heaven, and all this land that I have spoken of will I give unto your seed, and they shall inherit it for ever.* (Exodus 32:13)

In the area of Jordan, Moses gives a description of the lands promised by God to the Israelites, and acknowledges that it was, indeed, an oath from Him. From the Book of Deuteronomy:

> *⁷Turn you, and take your journey, and go to the mount of the Amorites, and unto all the places nigh thereunto, in the plain, in the hills, and in the vale, and in the south, and by the sea side, to the land of the Canaanites, and unto Lebanon, unto the great river, the river Euphrates. ⁸Behold, I have set the land before you: go in and possess the land which the LORD sware unto your fathers, Abraham, Isaac, and Jacob, to give unto them and to their seed after them.* (Deuteronomy 1:7-8)

Here we see that the Israelites are referred to as a "people of inheritance" as it relates to the land "over the Jordan."

> *²⁰But the LORD hath taken you, and brought you forth out of the iron furnace, even out of Egypt, to be unto him a people of inheritance, as ye are this day. ²¹Furthermore the LORD was angry with me for your sakes, and sware that I should not go over Jordan, and that I should not go in unto that good land, which the LORD thy God giveth thee for an inheritance: ²²But I must die in this land, I must not go over Jordan: but ye shall go over, and possess that good land.* (Deuteronomy 6:20-22)

Here is another reiteration of the oath given the Israelites from God pertaining to the land.

> *¹⁰And it shall be, when the LORD thy God shall have brought thee into the land which he sware unto thy fathers, to Abraham, to Isaac, and to Jacob, to give thee great and goodly cities, which thou buildedst not....* (Deuteronomy 6:10)

Next it is made clear that the Lord is not giving this land to the Israelites because they are so good, but because those possessing the land are so wicked. As such, He desires the Israelites to drive these people off of the land. He goes as far as to describe the Israelites as a *stiffnecked people.* But, most importantly, He once again states that He *sware the land to thy fathers, Abraham, Isaac, and Jacob.*

> *⁵Not for thy righteousness, or for the uprightness of thine heart, dost thou go to possess their land: but for the wickedness of these nations the LORD thy God doth drive them out from before thee, and that he may perform the word which the LORD sware unto thy fathers, Abraham, Isaac, and Jacob. ⁶Understand therefore, that the LORD thy God giveth thee not this good land to possess it for thy righteousness; for thou art a stiffnecked people.* (Deuteronomy 9:5-6)

Here is yet another passage in the Book of Deuteronomy confirming the oath given by the Lord of the land to the Israelites.

> *¹¹And the LORD said unto me, Arise, take thy journey before the people, that they may go in and possess the land, which I sware unto their fathers to give unto them.* (Deuteronomy 10:11)

Here we see the oath, then a description of the land's quality, that it is not like Egypt's land, and most interestingly of all, it is a land where *the eyes of the LORD thy God are always upon it, from the beginning of the year even unto the end of the year.* In other words, this particular plot of land on the entire Earth is special to God. As such He has given it to whom He wished.

> *⁹And that ye may prolong your days in the land, which the LORD sware unto your fathers to give unto them and to their seed, a land that floweth with milk and honey. ¹⁰For the land, whither thou goest in to possess it, is not as the land of Egypt, from whence ye came out, where thou sowedst thy seed, and wateredst it with thy foot, as a garden of herbs: ¹¹But the land, whither ye go to possess it, is a land of hills and valleys, and drinketh water of the rain of heaven: ¹²A land which the LORD thy God careth for: the eyes*

of the LORD thy God are always upon it, from the beginning of the year even unto the end of the year. (Deuteronomy 11:9-12)

After exhorting the Israelites concerning the land, He urges them to write His words on the posts of their houses, restating His oath.

²⁰And thou shalt write them upon the door posts of thine house, and upon thy gates: ²¹That your days may be multiplied, and the days of your children, in the land which the LORD sware unto your fathers to give them, as the days of heaven upon the earth. (Deuteronomy 11:20-21)

The words here show still more attachment to the land in question, the Lord describing what to do in honor of Him along with His oath.

²That thou shalt take of the first of all the fruit of the earth, which thou shalt bring of thy land that the LORD thy God giveth thee, and shalt put it in a basket, and shalt go unto the place which the LORD thy God shall choose to place his name there. ³And thou shalt go unto the priest that shall be in those days, and say unto him, I profess this day unto the LORD thy God, that I am come unto the country which the LORD sware unto our fathers for to give us. ⁴And the priest shall take the basket out of thine hand, and set it down before the altar of the LORD thy God. (Deuteronomy 26:2-4)

Here we see a description of His intention toward the land, along with His oath stated once again.

¹¹And the LORD shall make thee plenteous in goods, in the fruit of thy body, and in the fruit of thy cattle, and in the fruit of thy ground, in the land which the LORD sware unto thy fathers to give thee. ¹²The LORD shall open unto thee his good treasure, the heaven to give the rain unto thy land in his season, and to bless all the work of thine hand: and thou shalt lend unto many nations, and thou shalt not borrow. (Deuteronomy 28:11-12)

Here the Israelites are forewarned what could cause them to lose possession of the land, but not their ownership of it. This, of course, would eventually happen:

> [20]*That thou mayest love the LORD thy God, and that thou mayest obey his voice, and that thou mayest cleave unto him: for he is thy life, and the length of thy days: that thou mayest dwell in the land which the LORD sware unto thy fathers, to Abraham, to Isaac, and to Jacob, to give them.* (Deuteronomy 30:20)

In the process of possessing the land promised by God, Moses explains to Israel the role Joshua will play in it, and reiterated the oath again.

> [7]*And Moses called unto Joshua, and said unto him in the sight of all Israel, Be strong and of a good courage: for thou must go with this people unto the land which the LORD hath sworn unto their fathers to give them; and thou shalt cause them to inherit it.* (Deuteronomy 31:7)

The Lord explains that the land must be divided among the tribes of Israel, and restates the oath.

> [6]*Be strong and of a good courage: for unto this people shalt thou divide for an inheritance the land, which I sware unto their fathers to give them.* (Joshua 1:6)

Here, it is stated that the Lord will never *break my covenant with you.* Also, there is a warning concerning the inhabitants of the land. Of further interest, here is the statement that those in the land *shall be as thorns in your sides.* This, of course, is the circumstance the Israelis face today.

> [1]*And an angel of the LORD came up from Gilgal to Bochim, and said, I made you to go up out of Egypt, and have brought you unto the land which I sware unto your fathers; and I said, I will never*

break my covenant with you. ²And ye shall make no league with the inhabitants of this land; ye shall throw down their altars: but ye have not obeyed my voice: why have ye done this? ³Wherefore I also said, I will not drive them out from before you; but they shall be as thorns in your sides, and their gods shall be a snare unto you. Judges 2:1-3

In the Book of Jeremiah, the oath is restated.

⁵That I may perform the oath which I have sworn unto your fathers, to give them a land flowing with milk and honey, as it is this day. Then answered I, and said, So be it, O LORD. (Jeremiah 11:5)

In the Book of Ezekiel, the oath given by the Lord is stated as I lifted up mine hand. A description of the borders of the land is also given here, and it encompasses all of the current land possessed by Israel:

¹³Thus saith the Lord GOD; This shall be the border, whereby ye shall inherit the land according to the twelve tribes of Israel: Joseph shall have two portions. ¹⁴And ye shall inherit it, one as well as another: concerning the which I lifted up mine hand to give it unto your fathers: and this land shall fall unto you for inheritance. (Ezekiel 47:13-14)

These are some, but not all, of the passages wherein it is made clear that He promised the land to the Jews long ago and that it represents their inheritance forever. Essentially, the deed to the land has been given by God Himself to the descendents of Abraham, Isaac and Jacob, the Jews. It is a land where ancient Egypt suffered greatly for attempting to prevent them from reaching it. And now with Israel restored back to the same land, strangely, as efforts are made to remove them, great catastrophes "coincidental" to those efforts have been occurring.

THE FORETOLD SCATTERING OF THE JEWS

As the Jewish fighters continued to resist, the Roman legions continued to destroy them one-by-one, their strongholds falling to the overwhelming might of Rome. After having tired of the rebellious people living in the Roman province of Palestine, Rome finally sent 60,000 legions under the Roman general Titus to break the back of the Jews and take the fortified city of Jerusalem. After a terrible five-month siege, the Roman army prevailed, breaching the walls and entering the city. The Holy Temple, the center of Jewish worship and culture was destroyed in the process. Jewish historian Josephus Flavius, who lived during the time that the temple was destroyed, recounts its destruction.

> ... in hot pursuit right up to the Temple itself. Then one of the soldiers, without awaiting any orders and with no dread of so momentous a deed, but urged on by some supernatural force, snatched a blazing piece of wood and, climbing on another soldier's back, hurled the flaming brand through a low golden window that gave access, on the north side, to the rooms that surrounded the sanctuary. As the flames shot up, the Jews let out a shout of dismay that matched the tragedy; they flocked to the rescue, with no thought of sparing their lives or husbanding their strength; for the sacred structure that they had constantly guarded with such devotion was vanishing before their very eyes.[1]

Today, as a tourist seeks the Temple in Jerusalem, it is not to be found. Except for a portion of an outer wall that remains, there is no sign of the incredible edifice that once was. Interestingly, in the days that Jesus walked the streets of Jerusalem, he informed his disciples of the following:

> *[1]And as he went out of the temple, one of his disciples saith unto him, Master, see what manner of stones and what buildings are here! [2]And Jesus answering said unto him, Seest thou these great*

buildings? there shall not be left one stone upon another, that shall not be thrown down. (Mark 13:1-3)

After the fulfillment of that prophecy, an odyssey lay ahead for the surviving Jews, a scattering across the world, their nation destroyed. This defeat would represent a seminal moment in the history of Israel, as well as the Jew's possession of the lands promised them by God. Their dispersion from the land would be as terrible as any experienced by a people, literally being scattered across the world, forced to live in a multitude of countries. Here too, this terrible future was given to the Jews to know well in advance from a most unwelcomed prophecy.

> *[64] And the LORD shall scatter thee among all people, from the one end of the earth even unto the other; and there thou shalt serve other gods, which neither thou nor thy fathers have known, even wood and stone. [65] And among these nations shalt thou find no ease, neither shall the sole of thy foot have rest: but the LORD shall give thee there a trembling heart, and failing of eyes, and sorrow of mind: [66] And thy life shall hang in doubt before thee; and thou shalt fear day and night, and shalt have none assurance of thy life:* (Deuteronomy 28:64-66)

And again the words of Jesus, recorded in the New Testament Book of Luke:

> *[24] And they shall fall by the edge of the sword, and shall be led away captive into all nations: and Jerusalem shall be trodden down of the Gentiles, until the times of the Gentiles be fulfilled.* (Mark 21:24)

And from the Book of Jeremiah:

> *[16] I will scatter them also among the heathen, whom neither they nor their fathers have known: and I will send a sword after them, till I have consumed them.* (Jeremiah 9:16)

Here we are told their scattering will be among peoples whom neither they nor their fathers have known. In fact, the Jews were *scattered* across the world to every corner resulting in many of them living among peoples that they had never known. They are also warned by the prophet that the Lord will *send a sword after them*. This specific detail also was fulfilled with the *scattered* Jews experiencing countless pogroms across the world.

More from the Book of Ezekiel:

> *¹⁵And I will scatter thee among the heathen, and disperse thee in the countries, and will consume thy filthiness out of thee.* (Ezekiel 22:15)

As history records, the scattering of the Jews, dispersed among the nations of the world, did, indeed, take place lasing two thousand years. Amazingly, in spite of so cataclysmic an event happening to their nation and their people, the nation was restored in 1948. But here, too, the outcome was foretold. This from the Book of Isaiah:

> *¹¹And it shall come to pass in that day, that the Lord shall set his hand again the second time to recover the remnant of his people, which shall be left, from Assyria, and from Egypt, and from Pathros, and from Cush, and from Elam, and from Shinar, and from Hamath, and from the islands of the sea. ¹²And he shall set up an ensign for the nations, and shall assemble the outcasts of Israel, and gather together the dispersed of Judah from the four corners of the earth.* Isaiah 11:11-12 KJV

The passage points out that the recovering of the remnant of the Jews back to Israel will be the second time the Lord will have done it, the first taking place from the Babylonian captivity. He further specifies that He will *gather together...from the four corners of the Earth* the Jews back to their land.

Then, this prophecy from the Book of Ezekiel, referred to as the Valley of Dry Bones prophecy which demonstrates, perhaps better than any prophecy, the incredible restoration of the Jewish nation to the land of their ancestors.

THE VALLEY OF DRY BONES

¹The hand of the LORD was upon me, and carried me out in the spirit of the LORD, and set me down in the midst of the valley which was full of bones, ²And caused me to pass by them round about: and, behold, there were very many in the open valley; and, lo, they were very dry. (Ezekiel 37:1-2)

In his vision, the old prophet is shown a valley of dried-out old bones. Next, after asking Ezekiel if these bones could live, the Lord describes what He intends to do with them:

³And he said unto me, Son of man, can these bones live? And I answered, O Lord GOD, thou knowest. ⁴Again he said unto me, Prophesy upon these bones, and say unto them, O ye dry bones, hear the word of the LORD. ⁵Thus saith the Lord GOD unto these bones; Behold, I will cause breath to enter into you, and ye shall live: ⁶And I will lay sinews upon you, and will bring up flesh upon you, and cover you with skin, and put breath in you, and ye shall live; and ye shall know that I am the LORD. (Ezekiel 37:3-6)

Ezekiel does as he is told, and the results are fascinating with skin beginning to cover the old, dry bones:

⁷So I prophesied as I was commanded: and as I prophesied, there was a noise, and behold a shaking, and the bones came together, bone to his bone. ⁸And when I beheld, lo, the sinews and the flesh came up upon them, and the skin covered them above: but there was no breath in them. (Ezekiel 37:7-8)

After seeing the amazing sight of bodies forming around the old and dry bones, he is told what to do next and sees another amazing sight, *an exceeding great army:*

> [9]*Then said he unto me, Prophesy unto the wind, prophesy, son of man, and say to the wind, Thus saith the Lord GOD; Come from the four winds, O breath, and breathe upon these slain, that they may live.* [10]*So I prophesied as he commanded me, and the breath came into them, and they lived, and stood up upon their feet, an exceeding great army.* (Ezekiel 37:9-10)

Then God explains to the prophet what he just saw. After a complete loss of hope following the great scattering of the Jews across the world, God will bring them back to their own land to dwell in it once again:

> [11]*Then he said unto me, Son of man, these bones are the whole house of Israel: behold, they say, Our bones are dried, and our hope is lost: we are cut off for our parts.* [12]*Therefore prophesy and say unto them, Thus saith the Lord GOD; Behold, O my people, I will open your graves, and cause you to come up out of your graves, and bring you into the land of Israel.* [13]*And ye shall know that I am the LORD, when I have opened your graves, O my people, and brought you up out of your graves,* [14]*And shall put my spirit in you, and ye shall live, and I shall place you in your own land: then shall ye know that I the LORD have spoken it, and performed it, saith the LORD.* (Ezekiel 37:11-14)

The fulfillment of that prophecy took place on May 14, 1948, with the rebirth of Israel. After being scattered among the nations for two thousand years, the rebirth involved a war against vastly superior forces surrounding the Jews. Amazingly, in spite of the odds, they won, fulfilling the old prophetic words of a restored nation.

The ancient prophets warned the disobedient Jews that they would be *scattered among the nations.* This, of course, is exactly what happened to them as a people. But to give some hope for a future, the prophets tell them that they will be restored back in the land after *the times of the Gentiles be fulfilled.* We are told in The Valley of Dry Bones prophecy the specific reconstituting of the Jewish people back to becoming a nation again. It will be noted that history records the fulfillment of these prophecies down to specific details. Now, with the fulfillment of these prophecies, a question arises. What type of response from the Divine should be expected if mankind would attempt to reverse these promises? Also, it was indicated that Israel would be reborn after the times of *the Gentiles be fulfilled,* indicating the time of Israel has once again begun. This too might lead some to conclude a danger associated with removing the Promised Land from Israel.

So this leads us to the question if there have been more such "coincidences" since the global financial meltdown. In the following six chapters, the case will be presented that there have been three more, which represent a continuation of *The Israel Omen* warnings.

CHAPTER FOUR

The Gulf Oil Rig Disaster

N ot long after the Annapolis Middle East Peace Conference in November 2007 and the promising months that followed, time continued its march into 2008 and the U.S. Presidential campaign that year. American presidential campaigns have a way of placing Middle East peace efforts on hold, and the 2008 campaign was no exception. The two major party candidates that would ultimately emerge, Senator John McCain of Arizona and Senator Barack Obama of Illinois, would, over the course of that year, answer many questions concerning the Middle East conflict, as well as the Quartet's (*four horns*) peace efforts. But the well known tendency for politicians to be political, answering questions to satisfy specific groups but without intent, reigned supreme that year. With this tendency having been studied overseas, the players in the region, as well as the international community, waited patiently for the inauguration of the next U.S. president.

With the inauguration of the new president in January 2009, a new Israeli leader also entered the scene. In America, the election of Barack Obama to the presidency represented a lurch to the political left for an America that sought "change" from the previous eight years of the Bush

Administration. Although "change" was now the order of the day, U.S. policy in the Middle East was expected to essentially remain as it had, protective of Israel. With Obama now heading for the White House, it was believed that U.S. Mideast policy would continue to stand by Israel, insuring her safety in a very rough neighborhood. Having granted the various Jewish groups assurances and solemn promises of continued strong support for the Jewish state, the overwhelming majority of Jewish voters would cast their money, as well as their vote, to the Democratic nominee, lending their support in his effort to "transform America."

In Israel, where a national election had also just been held, it was a different story altogether. Just when America had moved to the political left, with both the executive and legislative branches now firmly in the hands of the most liberal elements of the Democratic Party, in Israel, the opposite took place. Having seen the bloody results of trying to compromise with radical Islam, particularly in Gaza, the Israeli electorate concluded they required a leader that would protect the nation first, a leader not prone to the bouts of naiveté of which his predecessors appeared to suffer. Seeking to place the safety of the nation above placating the international community and radical Islam, the Israeli electorate cast the majority of their votes for political parties on the ideological right, thus assuring that Likud leader Benjamin Netanyahu would become prime minister once again.

Having previously served as leader of Israel during the Clinton years, Netanyahu had earned a reputation for his unwillingness to compromise on Israeli security, making Clinton's effort to secure an agreement between the conflicted parties in the region all the more difficult. Now, just as another Democratic administration was taking power in Washington, so, too, was Netanyahu once again in Israel.

With an Israeli prime minister now in office from the political right, the "progress" made at Annapolis during the Quartet's (*four horns*) gathering there in 2007 receded into the shadows, extinguished by the reality that those previous efforts only emboldened enemies dedicated to fulfilling their own frightening version of a "final solution." Although the framework for a peace settlement had actually been established from that conference, as acknowledged by Quartet (*four horns*) envoy Tony Blair in early 2008, it required an Israeli prime minister willing to pursue it. That was something that now no longer existed. As a result "progress" was put on hold, much to the chagrin of the international community that gathered against the ancient "Promised Land" for the creation of a new Palestinian state.

Now the stage was set for a classic showdown between two ideological extremes, the liberal Obama Administration and the conservative, new Israeli government of Netanyahu. The showdown would not be long in coming. After the fanfare of the presidential inauguration ended, President Obama set out quickly to bring an unexpected "change" to American foreign policy in the Mideast and Israel in particular.

The new president would visit the Middle East to deliver his first major foreign policy speech at Cairo University in Egypt, not even bothering to visit Israel while in the area. But if that wasn't disturbing enough to the modern Israelites, he added coals to their fires of concern by again visiting the region, Turkey this time, and again avoiding the Jewish state.

* * * * * * *

For many living along the Gulf Coast, some of the most pleasant memories include time spent on its white beaches riding the Gulf's accommodating waves during summer vacations that were always too short. For some, it is memories of Santa Rosa Island just off the coast of Pensacola. For others, a different kind of Gulf Coast has always beckoned, one lapping at the Mississippi River Delta just inside the "coast," as it were, of southern Louisiana. Its countless waterways cut through the land, ultimately leading to the Gulf of Mexico, and represent a maze of secret fishing spots coveted by sportsmen. The rich delta soil, refined from its long, slow journey south, produces a food chain value that ultimately creates some of the best fishing in the world being rich with red fish, trout, crabs, and shrimp, many of which ultimately end up served by the best restaurants in New Orleans. Truly, it has been a sportsman's paradise for as long as memories extend.

The Louisiana economy feeds off of two natural resources, crude oil and seafood, with both located in great abundance just off the coast. A slow drive south from New Orleans, down highway 90 to Houma, Louisiana, and deep into Cajun country, would convince any skeptic these industries are significant. With "fresh shrimp" signs seen almost as frequently as those for oil field service companies, jobs in both industries are always viewed as options for local workers.

As April 2010 began, representing the last respite before the extreme heat of a south Louisiana summer, both industries continued humming along, confident in the insatiable appetite of the masses for all they could harvest. In the Gulf of Mexico, the realm where seafood and oil reign supreme, an engineering marvel had been probing the depths for crude oil, depths that had never before been reached. The "Deepwater Horizon" oil rig made drilling history in September 2009 by reaching an incredible drilling depth of 35,050 feet, the booty sought after by the $560 million rig was a pocket of oil believed to be one of the largest in the world on a lease owned by British Petroleum.[1]

* * * * * * *

Sometimes, a stroll down memory lane does good, allowing current events to be placed in proper perspective with the clarity of hindsight. As it pertains to the establishment of a Palestinian state, such a stroll is worth taking and begins in 1936. In that year the region called Palestine was still under control of Great Britain, which had ruled the highly contentious area since 1920, when it came into their possession from the recently vanquished Ottoman Empire. It was contentious because the Jews and Arabs living in the area could not get along, conflict being the norm rather than the exception. In an effort to finally bring an end to the tensions and constant killings, a royal commission headed by Lord Peel, British envoy to the troubled area, went to the region to investigate the causes of the conflict and find a solution. The solution he offered was simple, divide the area into an Arab state and a Jewish state based on the density of their populations. Peel concluded that "partition offers a chance of ultimate peace," and that "no other plan does."

With this solution in hand and an offer that would have brought to reality the Arab nation of Palestine in 1936, Arab leaders across the region turned it down cold. Their foremost leader, Palestinian Haj Amin al-Husseini, instead chose to align with Adolf Hitler and in return received assurances from the Nazi leader of a "free hand to eradicate every last Jew from Palestine, and the Arab world." Essentially, when given the choice between their own nation and conflict, the Palestinian Arabs chose conflict, the one that continues to this day.

In 1947, with Hitler gone and the United Nations now in charge of the area, another plan was presented to the Arabs. Again, it was offered that the Arabs and Jews of Palestine would each be given areas in the region based on their population density to create their own nation. Here too, instead of accepting the offer, and thus creating a Palestinian state in 1947, the leading Arab organization, the Arab League, voted to block the plan's implementation and instead wage "a war of extermination and a momentous massacre" against the Jews.

Some people believe that three chances to accept generosity is enough, the rejection representing the proverbial third strike. Just after the 1967 Six-Day War, which resulted in large tracts of the ancient "Promised

Land" falling under the control of Israel for the first time in 2,000 years, the Jewish state initially offered to return the land they had just captured in exchange for a peace agreement with the surrounding Muslim nations. But the vanquished would have none of it, and the offer was quickly and soundly rejected. The dramatic rejection came at the infamous Khartoum Arab Summit, their famous response recorded for history. At the conclusion of the summit, the unanimous gathering assured the world that there would be, "...no peace with Israel, no negotiations with Israel, no recognition of Israel," their third strike. Prior to that war, all of the lands now in contention had been available for the creation of a Palestinian state, if the nation of Jordan, who controlled the area had so desired. But no offer was forthcoming from the Jordanians. Only after Israel captured the land in 1967 did it become a cause of great concern to that Arab nation.

From the view of the Israelis who, in 1967, had struck the gathering Arab armies just prior to themselves being attacked, there was nobody on the other side of the great chasm to even talk to. As a result, Israel began building settlements all across the newly acquired lands, fulfilling ancient prophecy and providing a much needed buffer of protection against her dangerous neighbors. Various American Administrations after the 1967 war worried that the building of settlements on those lands, otherwise known as the "Promised Land," was harmful to chances for peace. But there were never any meaningful repercussions from doing so until 2010.

Hopeful that it would be his administration that would finally make history, scaling the slippery mountain the Mideast conflict represented to the world of diplomacy, Obama would embark on a campaign to pressure Israel into concessions for "peace," that had never before been accomplished by any previous U.S. Administration. In line with that pressure, as reported by the *New York Times* in April 2010, the President sent a letter to Palestinian President Abbas stating that unlike the past, should Israel do anything that in the view of Obama's administration undermined the peace process, the U.S. would no longer stand in the way of United Nations resolutions condemning it. The epicenter of U.S. concern, what it considered an action that would undermine the "peace" process, centered on the issuing of building permits for construction in East Jerusalem. This issue, which had never before kept the Palestinians from the negotiating table, was now added to their requirements for sitting down and talking, thanks to the new policy being enacted by the Obama administration.

Although the building permit issue had been one of contention between Israel and previous U.S. Administrations, by March 2010 it became a flashpoint for the most serious break in decades between the two allies. The spark that would ignite it came that month during an official visit to Israel by Vice President Joseph Biden. The announcement that a permit to construct 1600 apartments in East Jerusalem was delivered during his visit and created a firestorm between the two nations with the incident viewed by the Obama Administration as a great insult.[2]

Netanyahu, surprised by the severity of the U.S. reaction, initially appeared caught off guard, claiming he was unaware the permit was about to be approved. Later, after catching his breath, he pointed out what any close observer to the negotiations would have known: that Israel had been building in East Jerusalem for the last 40 years, and never before had America responded with such anger because of it. After all, the Prime Minister would say, it is a part of Israel. Indeed, according to the ancient Scriptures, the city was clearly given to the restored Israel by God Himself. Now, in the name of "peace," America was pressing hard to impact Israeli sovereignty over the Holy city, seeking to restrict development in the Eastern part as a first step toward ultimately seeing it become the capital of a future Palestinian state. Never in the decades since Israel had acquired East Jerusalem had building or settling it ceased. The efforts to develop and settle East Jerusalem had always progressed, unmoved by requests from the United States to stop construction. But now there was something quite different about the current U.S. requests, this Administration meant it and was willing to begin removing its support from the small Jewish state to get it. That support was viewed by many as vital for the very existence of the nation. As Roger Cohen, op-ed columnist for *The New York Times* would write, "Obama's recalibration of U.S. Middle East diplomacy is ground-shifting," and indeed it was.[3]

Former U.S. Senator George Mitchell, Mideast envoy for presidents Clinton, Bush and then Obama, would say, "There has never been in the White House a president that is so committed on this issue, including Clinton who is a personal friend, and there will never be, at least in the lifetimes of anyone in this room."[4] As most observers to the Mideast conflict knew this profound observation from a player at the center of the storm was accurate, Obama was beginning a shift in U.S. policy against Israel intended to pressure the Jews into relinquishing Israeli control over the city Ezekiel had foretold over 2500 years ago would be returned to the restored nation.

* * * * * * *

As is common with oil rigs operating in the Gulf of Mexico, sundry service companies perform various duties for the rig's owner, and in this case for British Petroleum (BP), the Deepwater Horizon was no different. After drilling for oil was complete, the job to "cement" each new segment of the well into place was awarded to Halliburton, one of the largest oil service related companies in the world. The job of cementing is one of the last jobs preformed after a drilling rig has struck oil or gas.[5] The decision to begin the "cementing" process for Deepwater Horizon had begun in early April, indicating the enormous rig would soon be finishing drilling, its job in the oil field known as "Mississippi Canyon 252" complete. The timing could not have been better for BP. On March 8 the British oil giant had applied to move the massive rig to drill in another oil field since the current operation was almost complete.[6] But the cementing job had taken longer than expected with concerns that the cement used, one mile under the Gulf surface had been contaminated with mud and thus diluting its effectiveness.

The first sign that the drilling operation was experiencing a problem occurred in late March. Mike Williams, the rig's chief electronics technician, noticed that chunks of rubber from a gasket that fit around the drill pipe had broken loose. The gasket insured that loose oil and gas would not escape, and create a volatile situation far below the surface. When he brought to the attention of his supervisor what he had seen, he was assured it was no big deal. Williams thought to himself, "How can it be no big deal, there's chunks of our seal now missing!"[7] That broken seal would ultimately become the first of several abnormalities experienced by the rig just as it was completing its great task at sea. It would be the first harbinger of a tragic day yet to come, one that would change the lives of countless people, making history in the worst way.

* * * * * * *

The crisis in U.S.-Israeli relations would reach its zenith during a visit by Netanyahu to the White House on March 23, 2010, a visit designed to placate the angry Obama Administration. Unlike leaders from nations across the world who are greeted at the opulent White House front door by either the President or Vice President, the Israeli leader would be required to enter the White House through the "back door," an entrance usually reserved for leaders of rogue nations. A minor presidential assistant would be there to greet him. However, after that inauspicious beginning, the snubs would increase. Later in the day Netanyahu would be left to "roam the White House," reportedly unattended, as the president left his "guest" to dine with the First Family. With this studied snub of the uncooperative Israeli leader, the White House had made its point, and the Israelis finally got it. Netanyahu's discomfort would increase during that visit with the announcement from Israel on March 24 that another apartment complex to be built in East Jerusalem had just been approved.

Diplomatic protocol is the art of fine detail, reflecting the official state of relations between nations as their representatives meet. For Israel the state of relations with the U.S. had always been strong. It was a relationship officially started with President Truman after David Ben-Gurian declared the nation's independence in 1948. Truman recognized the new state fifteen minutes later. From that point forward, friendship between the two nations grew deeper. But, in 1991, something began to change, if only slightly at first. The United States, increasingly sensitive to its growing oil dependence, began to believe that to secure its position with the oil rich nations in the Mideast, it was necessary to pressure the Jewish State to return the lands acquired in the 1967 war. In 1991, when the first Bush Administration had successfully gathered the parties to the Mideast conflict at the Madrid Conference, the Arab side was assured that his administration was doing everything it could to ultimately bring about the return of the lands captured in 1967. From that point forward, the U.S. relationship with Israel began taking on a more rocky nature, but one still between friends. It was, however, from that year that historically severe catastrophes began taking place with timing eerily associated with efforts to remove the ancient lands.[8] Sensing that a serious break was occurring in the relationship for the first time, pressure within the Israeli government to repair it became palpable.

It was made clear to the Netanyahu government that, in order to continue having good relations with the U.S., it would be necessary for Israel to cease construction in East Jerusalem. This requirement, however, was one that had never before been demanded by any U.S. president as a prerequisite to good relations. That would present a serious political problem for the prime minister of Israel.

The elevation of Netanyahu to the office of Prime Minister had been the result of various political parties from the political right combining their votes to provide a majority, enabling a government to be formed by Likud, headed by Netanyahu. In order to gain the cooperation of certain parties, and their much needed support, Netanyahu had to agree with their positions on various issues of critical importance to them. One central issue for many in his governing coalition was East Jerusalem. Simply stated, they would not tolerate a construction freeze in the Holy city. Of course, it was necessary for construction permits to continue being issued so housing units could continue being built and settlers could continue moving in. A cessation of issuing building permits would effectively stop the growth of settlements in East Jerusalem, something no Israeli Prime minister had ever agreed to. But from the viewpoint of the new Obama Administration, such a cessation would represent a breakthrough for "peace." To many Israelis such an action would represent a violation of a promise to Israel from God Himself, assuring them that Jerusalem was to be theirs.

In April, with negotiations between the Israelis and Palestinians having been in a state of suspension for 16 months, the U.S. administration knew what was required to get the Palestinians back to the table. For the Israelis, no conditions existed in order to sit and talk. But for the Palestinians, a new condition had emerged, one actually placed in the process by the U.S. Administration. Taking the lead from Obama, the Palestinians declared, unequivocally, that unless there was a construction freeze in East Jerusalem, they would under no circumstances return to the talks.

Within Israel, many on the political right found the new demand from America, and now the Palestinian side, completely unacceptable. Israel had always built in East Jerusalem and never before did it prevent negotiations from taking place. Now, with international pressure to stop building in East Jerusalem led by the United States, leaders across the political spectrum within Israel began speaking out. Right-wing lawmakers in the Knesset began praising Netanyahu for standing firm, refusing the

Obama administration's demand to freeze construction. On the other side of the political spectrum, fear was expressed that it was a big mistake to alienate the nation's most powerful ally. That sentiment was best summed-up by the leader of the leftist-Meretz party, who stated "Netanyahu has said no to the peace process, aggravating the rift with the American administration." The right-wing National Religious Party Chairman, Daniel Herskovitz, in support of Netanyahu, stated that his rejection of Obama's pressure represented an "appropriate Zionist response."

The Independent newspaper would report on April 23, 2010, "Israeli Prime Minister Benjamin Netanyahu has rejected US demands to freeze Jewish construction in East Jerusalem, creating a key stumbling block to renewed peace talks...." Quoting the Prime Minister, "I am saying one thing. There will be no freeze in Jerusalem."[8]

With Netanyahu once again resisting pressure to stop building in East Jerusalem, it appeared that the new requirement for resuming peace talks had been resisted. The Jews would continue building in East Jerusalem. At least that's how it appeared on the surface. But sometimes appearances can be deceiving, especially when it comes to the Middle East.

* * * * * * *

At 11:00 a.m., on the day that would become infamous, Doug Brown, chief mechanic on Deepwater Horizon, attended a "standard" planning meeting with other managers of the project, including the BP "company man" Robert Kaluza, considered the site leader for the project, along with his fellow Transocean employee Jimmy Harrell, the rig's offshore installation manager. However, the meeting was anything but standard, with a "skirmish" breaking out between Kaluza on one side, and Harrell, Brown, and the rig's driller lined up on the other side. As the chain of command went, Transocean had been hired by BP to operate the rig and therefore, ultimately, took orders from Kaluza. The dispute occurred when the driller began outlining what would take place to finalize the operation and to cap the well so another rig could later come to tap the tremendous reserves of oil and gas that had been successfully plumbed. The Transocean driller advised the gathering that "heavy mug" would be used in the "riser." The riser is the pipe that connects the rig to the actual oil well on the seabed. By using "heavy mud" instead of seawater it would take longer to complete the job, but was a much safer method since the mud would be able to better restrain the pressure within the riser. However, Kaluza insisted on replacing the heavy, protective mud within the riser, with much lighter sea water.[10]

The problem with such an approach is simple. Heavy protective mud was typically required in order to offset the tremendous pressure of oil trying to push to the surface before its time. Seawater, on the other hand, being much lighter than the "mud" could possibly give way to the primordial forces being tapped, resulting in the rig blowing. As the driller was speaking, Kaluza interrupted, settling the issue. "No, we'll be having some changes to that." He went on to explain that in place of the heavier "mud," seawater would instead be used. At this point, the Transocean men knew that this was anything but proper procedure, which raised serious concerns. But their protests would be cut short, Kaluza assuring them, "This is how it is going to be." Since it was BP that had hired Transocean the three would reluctantly, and fatefully, agree. As the three Transocean, employees left the infamous meeting, Jimmy Harrell would tell Brown, "Well, I guess that's what we have "pinchers" for." His words would be prophetic.[11]

The "pinchers" Harrell was referring to were shear rams on the blowout preventer, a device designed to slice through the drill pipe in a final, desperate act to close off a runaway well. But although it was an important safety device, it was not one any rig wanted to have to rely upon.

* * * * * *

With the apparent deadlock in negotiations due to the East Jerusalem building issue, it appeared there was no good reason for the Obama Mideast envoy George Mitchell to return to Israel anytime soon. Then suddenly it was announced on Wednesday, April 21 that the presidential envoy would return, set to arrive in just two days, on Friday, April 23. The announcement was especially interesting since it had been made clear that Mitchell would not return unless there was a good reason. Under the current circumstances the only good reason would be if Israel agreed to stop construction in East Jerusalem. Adding more mystery to Mitchell's sudden announcement had been a statement earlier in the month by U.S. State Department spokesman J.P. Crowley. Crowley, speaking on the possibility of another trip to the Middle East by Mitchell, made it clear that, "We don't go to meet just to meet. We go because we have some indication that both sides are willing to engage seriously on the issues that are on the table."[12] At this point in time from the U.S. perspective, "engaging seriously" meant that Israel must relent on Obama's new East Jerusalem requirement.

The first sign that the Israeli government's emphatic rejection of a building freeze in East Jerusalem might not be completely accurate came from the most unlikely of sources. Of the various small political parties that combined their votes to make Benjamin Netanyahu prime minister in early 2009, perhaps the most far-right was the Shas party. Led by its controversial religious leader, Rabbi Ovadiah Yosef, its position on East Jerusalem was clear, that the city was given to Israel by God, and it must not be divided. As such, the Shas party was not in favor of the establishment of a Palestinian state, nor for ceasing Jewish construction in East Jerusalem.[13] As a political force within the current government, anything less than a united Jerusalem under Israeli sovereignty was unacceptable, the violation of which could cause Shas to pull out of the Netanyahu coalition, and bring down his government.

As perhaps the leading ultra-Orthodox religious political party in Israel, that position was expected. With Jerusalem being Holy to Jews of faith, it was not an issue ripe for compromise. But what was not expected by Yosef was a statement he made during Mitchell's hastily arranged April 23 visit. As reported by one of Israel's largest newspapers, *Ma'ariv,* Yosef indicated that he believed Israel could afford to suspend construction in East Jerusalem, if it would help preserve the US-Israeli relationship. The paper went on to report that the influential Rabbi's remarks were made during a conversation with Israeli President Shimon Perez.[14] As one of the most far-right of Netanyahu's coalition partners, the statement surprised many.

Almost immediately after Mitchell's visit concluded, reports began surfacing that the long stalled "proximity talks" would soon start again. Those talks had not taken place for over 16 months, with the Palestinian side assuring the world they would not talk without Israel abiding by Obama's new condition, the suspension of construction in East Jerusalem. In an organization that glorifies giving one's life in order to kill an enemy of the Palestinian people, its leaders must take great care not to carelessly accommodate Israel. Returning to the negotiating table without a significant Israeli concession was not a viable option. Simply put, the Palestinians had the support of the President of the United States on the East Jerusalem issue, and also observed that as Israel opposed that new U.S. demand, relations between the two declined. Knowing that the focal point of the problem between the two was the Israeli refusal to stop construction in East Jerusalem, as far as the Palestinian side was concerned, they could sit back and wait, allowing their enemy to stew in the juices of their own decisions. The Palestinian side knew that returning to the "proximity talks" without the East Jerusalem concession would be letting the Israelis off the hook, an action seen as a betrayal against the cause of Palestine, alleviating the distress of the enemy as pressure was building on him. As such, it was the Israeli side that had to move because the President of the United States had made this issue his own.

Internet news report on April 25 by FoxNews.com titled, "Signs of progress as Obama envoy wraps up mission," stated that Mitchell would return to the region the very next week, indicating some kind of progress had been made during his sudden April 23 trip.[15] Later, on April 28 the British newspaper *The Guardian* indicated in an online article titled, "Israel and Palestinians close to restarting peace talks," that indirect talks, "proximity talks," mediated by the United States, would likely begin in a couple of weeks. The article went on to acknowledge that the talks would be the first since late 2008, just before the Israeli military incursion into Gaza in their attempt to stop rocket attacks into Israel. Interestingly, it was further indicated in the article that "Comments from both sides suggest an informal understanding has been reached about the issue of Jewish settlements building in Jerusalem." Indeed, whatever understanding was reached was quite informal, with the Netanyahu government continuing to declare no freeze would be implemented, yet the Palestinians satisfied enough to return to the talks.

Finally, on May 9, the Palestinians officially announced the start of "proximity talks" after almost a year and a half of being suspended. The talks were planned to last four months with Mitchell shuttling between the parties during that time. According to Mohammed Daraghmeh, writing in the political journal *Real Clear Politics*, in his article titled "Palestinians: Indirect peace talks have begun," the resumption of peace talks represented the first concrete achievement for the Obama administration in that region of the world since taking office.[16]

* * * * * * *

At 5:00 p.m. a sharp fall in fluid levels in the riser pipe was observed. This, the crew knew, was serious. It indicated a leak in the critical rubber gasket that closes tightly around the drill pipe, the same rubber gasket that several weeks earlier Mike Williams had brought to the attention of his superior who assured him it was nothing to worry about.[17]

By 6:00 p.m. it was discovered that a critical pressure test had been performed with the results indicating the existence of "a very large abnormality". But the crew, ignoring the warning, continued on with the process, a "fundamental mistake" that would prove to be a fatal one.[18]

Then, ominously, a sharp increase in fluid level began coming out of the well at about 9:00 p.m., after the crew had begun withdrawing the seawater used to suppress the great pressures surging upward from deep below the surface. In an effort to arrest the growing problem, and prevent the rig from blowing, the crew then shut down the pumps that were being used to withdraw the seawater, but to no avail. At this point it was obvious that the rig was experiencing a "kick," an uncontrollable surge in pressure from oil and gas deep down in the well, and a very dangerous sign. It was a clear indication that the well was now out of control. Now, events began to take control, with eleven crew members and the rig that had broken the drill depth record having less than an hour of life remaining.[19]

* * * * * * *

In politics, informal arrangements have a way of becoming public especially when engaged on an international level. As early as Tuesday, April 27, the day after Mitchell departed the region, Steven Hurst, reporting in *Real Clear Politics* stated that:

> Word emerged Monday (April 26) that the Israeli government had effectively frozen Jewish construction in Jerusalem's disputed eastern sector. In short order Palestinian President Mahmoud Abbas signaled he again would be ready to start indirect talks with Israel. The sudden change in direction was a victory for Obama's beleaguered Mideast envoy George Mitchell, who

had spent more than a year in private talks and repeated trips to Jerusalem and Ramallah.

Hurst would go on to say that:

Obama, from the earliest days of his presidency, had joined the Palestinians in demanding that Israel halt construction of more housing in the disputed eastern sector of the city. Netanyahu routinely, bluntly refused.

Netanyahu's refusal was in line with the promises, recorded in the ancient Hebrew Scriptures, and it was also the position Israeli Prime Ministers had taken as long as anyone could remember. But something had indeed changed. Soon, other news outlets began picking up on the reality that something was happening in East Jerusalem. Amy Tiebel, writing for the Associated Press, noted, "Israel's Prime Minister has effectively frozen new Jewish construction in East Jerusalem."

CNN reported that a Jerusalem city councilman with contacts in the building department indicated that there has been a "direct order" against building in East Jerusalem since Vice President Joe Biden's visit the previous month. Quoting Councilman Meir Margalit of the left-leaning Meretz Party, "Since the day Biden came here, there is a direct order not to permit Jewish building in East Jerusalem until further announcement." Continuing, he noted, "At the Interior Ministry, all meetings of the Regional Committee for Planning and Building have been suspended." He went on to add, "All of this was ordered orally, not in writing. The Interior Ministry would deny this, and that would be unequivocally false."[20]

More reports from the *Associated Press* reiterated the freeze, again stating that

Israel's Prime Minister has effectively frozen new Jewish construction in east Jerusalem, municipal officials said Monday, reflecting the need to mend a serious rift with the U.S. and get Mideast peace talks back on track. [21]

With the benefit of hindsight, it is now apparent that the Netanyahu government, in an effort to placate the estranged Obama Administration, relented to demands that it cease issuing construction permits in East Jerusalem. Additionally, it appears Israeli efforts to establish the freeze began not long after Biden's disastrous visit in March, with the new, secret Israeli concession ready to be offered by late April.[22]

On April 25 *Haaretz News* reported that Israeli and U.S. diplomats had been holding secret talks just prior to Mitchell's visit. Then, quite tellingly, the BBC reported why on April 21 Mitchell suddenly decided to return to Israel on such short notice:

> The US State Department spokesman indicated Mr. Mitchell only decided on the visit to the Middle East on Wednesday evening, after talks other US officials had held in Israel in the proceeding days suggested it would be "fruitful" for Mr. Mitchell to travel.[23][24]

Now a timeline of events leading to the breakthrough can be constructed, a breakthrough that for the first time since Israel's prophetic re-establishment as a nation would reduce Israeli sovereignty over Jerusalem. The above announcement from the State Department made it clear that the decision for Mitchell to return to Israel was made on Wednesday, April 21. In the aftermath of that visit, the Associated Press would begin reporting that a de facto construction permit freeze in East Jerusalem was in place. The Associated Press report confirmed indications by "other U.S. officials" engaged in secret talks with the Israelis that it would finally be "fruitful" for Mitchell to return. At that point in time, "fruitful," from a U.S. diplomatic standpoint, could only mean one thing, Israel was relenting on the East Jerusalem demand, again confirmed by Associated

Press reports. The statement also indicates the breakthrough came in the "preceding days." In other words, the Israeli decision to give in to U.S. demands concerning East Jerusalem took place sometime just prior to April 21, the "preceding days." Considering Mitchell had experienced no success after 16 months of efforts, it is doubtful once the de facto freeze was finally offered to the "other U S officials" it would take very long for Mitchell's decision to return to be made. Therefore, the most logical time frame that Israel offered to the "other U S officials," to effectively reduce their sovereignty over East Jerusalem is April 20, 2010.

* * * * * * *

Mike Enzell, Transocean senior tool-pusher was just settling in to sleep when a call came in from the drill floor. Enzell had hours earlier turned over control of the drilling operations to his relief, Jason Anderson. Now at 9:50 p.m. the voice on the other end of the line sounded worried. "We have a situation, the well is blowing out, we have mud going to the crown." The voice was Steve Curtis, the assistant driller. Horrified, Ezell asked if the well had been "shut in," a desperate final act that could end the crisis. Curtis told him that Jason Anderson was in the process of doing just that. Ezell, assuring Curtis he was on his way to help them, began quickly getting dressed. However, he would never make it back to the drill floor.[25]

Grabbing his boots so he could hasten to their assistance, a sudden explosion threw him clear across the room and against the bulkhead. Almost instantly, heavy smoke filled the quarters that only moments earlier he was settling down to sleep in. He could feel droplets of methane now on his face and could hear cries for help within the smoky nightmare. He hoped, he had, in fact, fallen asleep and this was a bad dream.[26]

Jimmy Harrell, who hours earlier had debated the plan insisted on by Kaluza, the BP company man in charge of the rig, now found himself on the bridge of a rescue ship after escaping the burning wreckage that had been a rig only minutes earlier. On the boat, Harrell was in contact with company officials via satellite phone. In an animated conversation he angrily challenged the party on the other end of the line screaming, "Are you f... happy? Are you f... happy? The rig is on fire! I told you this was going to happen." Harrell paused, the party on the other end of the line apparently attempting to calm him, then from Harrell "I am f...calm you realize the rig is burning?" Then, sensing a situation that could get out of control, the ship's captain asked Herrell to leave the bridge of the ship.[27]

After becoming the first rig to plumb depths never before reached, Deepwater Horizon began sinking to the deep bottom of the Gulf of Mexico, finding its oily grave a mile below the surface next to its prodigy, the well whose life would continue to uncontrollably defile the Gulf of Mexico in the ensuing months. The result would be the twin industries of oil and seafood being brought to their knees, representing one of the worst ecological disasters in history. The rig explosion and its terrible impact would live on in the memories of all affected, along with the date April 20, 2010.

CHAPTER FIVE

The Iceland Volcano

Across the world there are numerous majestic cities that stand out in their significance to western culture and history. The cities of Rome, Paris, and London readily come to mind with millions of visitors each year testifying to this truth. But few cities capture the imagination of both east and west like Jerusalem. Located in the Judean hills of Israel, it is a city that touches a multitude of people, crossing lines of culture, history and faith. Of all that Jerusalem has to offer, and it is much, it is The Old City that captures the attention of the faiths of the world. Covering roughly 220 acres, it is surrounded by walls ordered built by the Ottoman Sultan, Suleiman the Magnificent in 1537. Within it are many of the world's most significant religious and historical sites. The Old City has eleven gates of entry, including the "Golden Gate" where, according to Jewish tradition, it is believed the Messiah will enter through when he comes to Jerusalem. Suleiman, understanding this tradition, sealed the gate during his rule.[1]

The main entrance to The Old City is the Jaffa Gate, which means "The Beloved," and refers to Abraham, the father of Judaism, Christianity, and Islam. The city is divided into four neighborhoods: the Muslim Quarter, Jewish Quarter, Armenian Quarter and the Christian Quarter.

Within the Jewish Quarter stood the Second Temple, built by King Solomon and destroyed in 70 A.D. by the Roman army after a revolt by the Jewish people against the yoke of Rome failed. A small part of the old temple remains and is considered by Jews across the world as sacred. The Western Wall, located at the Temple Mount was an outer wall of the ancient temple, and is considered by Jews to be their most significant place of worship. Along with the glittering gold of the Dome of the Rock, it is one of the most recognizable images of Jerusalem.[2]

It is the image of the Western Wall that is often used by the Israeli Government Tourist Office to lure foreigners to visit Israel, most with lots of cash in their pockets to spend. Because of the historical and religious importance of Jerusalem, tourism provides a significant economic boost to the Jewish nation, and without such revenue, the nation would not be as prosperous. It was therefore, well within the norm of Israeli tourist promotion posters sent overseas to use images of the famous wall in an effort to promote tourism.

Within the United Kingdom, there is a governmental entity called the Advertising Standards Authority (ASA). It is the responsibility of the ASA to make sure that advertising is not deceptive, or misleading, protecting the public from the unscrupulous. The following statement represents the broad Advertising Code the ASA board members are to be governed by:

> The Advertising Codes contain wide-ranging rules designed to ensure that advertising does not mislead, harm or offend. Ads must also be socially responsible and prepared in line with the principles of fair competition. These broad principles apply regardless of the product being advertised.[3]

In early 2010, the Israeli Government was using a tourist promotional poster featuring the Western Wall as one of its photos in an advertisement campaign inside Great Britain. Under the photo, it stated "YOU CAN TRAVEL THE LENGTH OF ISRAEL IN 6 HOURS."

The ASA received one complaint, just one, in late March 2010. It centered on the photo of the Western Wall, and that since that ancient Israeli structure was within Eastern Jerusalem, the complaint claimed it was not Israeli territory, but "occupied" territory. Therefore, the complainant urged, that the poster was misleading and would leave the unsuspecting public with the notion that East Jerusalem was a part of Israel.

Within the ancient Hebrew Scriptures the old words assure a doubting world that those who meddle with Jerusalem will face the wrath of God. From chapter twelve of the Book of Zechariah:

And in that day will I make Jerusalem a burdensome stone for all people: all that burden themselves with it shall be cut in pieces, though all the people of the earth be gathered together against it. (Zechariah 12:2)

On April 14, 2010, the ASA rendered its decision, agreeing that the ad was misleading because it depicted East Jerusalem as a part of Israel, upholding the complaint, and resulting in the removal of the advertisement. The decision was clear, stating that, "The ad must not be shown again in its current form."[4] On April 14, as the ASA was busy issuing its ruling against Israeli possession of East Jerusalem, something just north of the British Islands began to awaken.

* * * * * * *

Deep within the recesses of the Earth move flows of lava and tectonic plates, primordial forces of nature capable of incredible power and destruction, and operating within their own time frame. Together, both are capable of creating land masses, and then moving them at will. Fortunately, neither acts with much frequency, but when they do the results can be devastating. In late March, as the ASA began its process of considering the complaint against the Israeli tourist poster, a volcano just north of Britain suddenly became active. On March 20, alkali-olivine basalt lava began flowing from various eruptive vents on the flanks of the old volcano Eyjafjallajokull. That lava flow would continue, watched by volcanic scientists for any indication that an eruption might be near.

Then, on April 14 as the ASA was issuing its decision against the Israeli advertisement, an indirect indictment of Israeli control over East Jerusalem, the Icelandic volcano began a major eruption, the like of which had not been seen since 1921, and before that 1821, and before that in 1612. It was a massive eruption that would, over the course of the following days, spew an estimated 250 million cubic metres of ejected ash, dust, and cinders into the atmosphere.

The direction of the jet stream just happened to be unusually stable at the time of the eruption, causing the ash plume created by the bellowing mammoth to drift toward the southwest. Having risen into the atmosphere to a height of 30,000 feet, the massive plume of ash and cinder created a blanket of ash so thick over the skies of Britain, and so quickly, that air travel in and out of the country had to be suspended the very next day, April 15.

But the impact of the prehistoric giant would not limit its reach to Britain alone, eventually spreading across most of Europe and bringing air travel to a halt across the entire continent. It would be the greatest disruption to air travel in Europe since World War II, bringing tourism across Britain and the continent to a grinding halt. The tourist cost to Britain alone would reach into the hundreds of millions of dollars.

Perhaps it was all just another odd coincidence, the like of which have been happening since 1991. That is possible. But as these coincidences continue to mount, perhaps, so should the doubt that they are only coincidences. In the following year, 2011, the effort to remove the Promised Land from Israel would enter a very new and aggressive phase. That story of the final "coincidence" takes some effort to properly tell, and is covered in the next four chapters.

CHAPTER SIX

The Pincer Movement

I t was the most odious regime in modern history, recognized by its twisted symbol and the fanatical man called the "leader." To most people in the world, the word "Nazi" brings forth a flood of horrific thoughts, usually accompanied by the question of how people could do such things to other people. Eventually, the monster that was its "leader" finally died. But before he breathed his last, he had taken to the grave almost 25 million people with him. To him even the lives of his soldiers appeared inconsequential. When one of his armies sent to conquer the Soviet Union was surrounded during the battle of Stalingrad, with no hope of winning that battle, there was a brief opportunity for them to escape certain annihilation. Instead, he passed on the opportunity to save them, ordering a fight to the death. They did, and the entire army was lost.

After a rampage of murder through the bread basket of the Soviet Union, his troops reached all the way to the outskirts of Moscow. He was stopped there, having come within a hair of knocking out the Soviet monolith, a victory that would have assured him complete domination of the old world. France, whose politicians appeared ready to stop him while he was still small and weak, looked for a willing partner in the lone superpower of that day, Great Britain. But at Number 10 Downing Street, they only found weakness. The leadership of that island nation had become too steeped in the idea of appeasement, believing if they gave in repeatedly to his demands, no matter how unreasonable, Hitler would leave them alone.

Czechoslovakia, the last of the smaller states to be given to the Nazi warlord without a fight, remains a diplomatic embarrassment to the British government to this day. After Hitler marched into the Rhineland, and later incorporated Austria into the Reich through intimidation, he turned his attention to the Czechs. The Czech Republic, a true democracy within Central Europe, became his target in the spring of 1938. The Western powers, led by Britain, reacted with alarm to the latest German threat of war. To avoid a potential conflict, leaders from Britain, Germany, France, and Italy met in Munich, Germany. The result of the much anticipated "peace" conference was shameful. In the end, the British demanded of their faithful ally to give up a large portion of their land to those that meant them ill. Accompanying the demand was a threat that if they did not, they would stand alone in the event of war with Germany.

Once the land was turned over, the Czech borders became indefensible, resulting in other neighboring countries, Hungary and Poland, demanding parts of the once proud republic. Within a month of the much hailed Munich Peace Conference, Czechoslovakia ceased to exist, doomed by its friendship to the lone superpower of that day.

Not long after Hitler consumed Czechoslovakia, he turned his attention to Poland, who had just helped cannibalize the unfortunate Czechs. Poland would soon fall to the Nazis with whom they had so recently colluded, and the next year France would fall. Britain, having stood aside as ally after ally was lost to the Nazis, was now isolated and alone. The German air force, the Luftwaffe, would punish the Brits badly in the beginning of the war. Then, as Hitler planned to invade the British Isles, his attention suddenly was diverted toward the Soviet Union, which he chose to invade instead. Though she had betrayed her allies, Britain had been spared, but just barely.

* * * * * * *

In the art of warfare there is a maneuver called the "pincer movement," and it is accomplished when an enemy is assaulted from opposite sides, and eventually surrounded. The first detailed account of its use comes to us from 216 B.C. when Hannibal, leading the army of Carthage, used it in defeating the superior forces of Rome. After drawing the Roman army into the center of his forces, Hannibal began to spread his army out and around the Roman flanks, eventually enveloping them. Once that was accomplished, the army of Rome was trapped and then massacred. Since that time, the pincer movement has been studied and occasionally used.

As 2011 began, it was becoming apparent that the Middle East conflict was experiencing a dramatic shift in the forces arrayed against Israel. Since the conflict's beginning, the Israelis had always faced the combined weight of the Arab world, all 200 million of them. However, in spite of those overwhelming numbers, the small Jewish state possessed the proverbial ace-in-the-hole, the unwavering support of the United States. Each president since Truman appeared to instinctively understand the tenuous nature of Israel's position, existing in a neighborhood surrounded by deadly enemies whose suicidal religious duty was to kill Jews. It was also apparent, from the history of those neighbors that their efforts went beyond only threats. That knowledge appeared to create a shared moral creed among American leaders for decades, knowing the U.S. might be the only force standing in the way of a second Holocaust. But with the election of Barack Obama in 2008, a major shift in the Middle East conflict would begin to take place. And, by 2011, it became apparent that

Hannibal's pincer movement tactic was being used to surround Israel diplomatically, and more importantly, militarily.

* * * * * * *

It is the norm in diplomacy that when a neutral party is called on to assist in settling a dispute, the positions of the conflicted parties must first be established. Once that is done, the diplomat sets out to narrow the differences between them. The effort takes time, and often progress is very slow, if at all. But over time, as their respective positions are nudged closer toward each other, a legitimate chance of settling the dispute may present itself. Obviously, the negotiator in the process must be careful to never do anything that widens the gulf of differences between the parties.

During the Clinton Administration, a master in the art of diplomacy was discovered in former Senator George Mitchell. Appointed by Clinton to find a peaceful resolution to the fighting in Northern Ireland, a conflict drenched in blood and hate for generations, Mitchell headed for the British Isles. His masterful and painstaking efforts to resolve that conflict took many years, patiently nudging the parties away from their hardened positions until, finally, both sides were close enough that an agreement could be signed. That document, the amazing Belfast Peace Agreement, was signed on Good Friday 1998.[1] America had found its diplomat, and the whole key to his success had been getting the conflicted parties to talk.

Not long after that success, Clinton would appoint Mitchell to seek a resolution to the Middle East conflict. Having achieved the impossible in Northern Ireland, he was the obvious choice to untie the Gordian knot of the next impossible problem. His effort began in earnest in 2000 when he headed a commission to investigate the causes of the conflict. He continued to serve during the eight years of the Bush administration, shuttling between Washington and Israel numerous times, negotiating between the parties, attempting to narrow the distance between their positions. Then, as President Obama took control in Washington, Mitchell stayed on in the same capacity.

However, early in the new administration, something strange began to take place in the Middle East negotiating process. Instead of attempting to narrow the gaping distance separating the Israeli and Palestinian positions, the president took a step that actually widened it. The issue centered on the building of Israeli housing in East Jerusalem. Since the 1967 Six-Day War, the Israelis had built apartment complexes and other housing in East Jerusalem. Although the Palestinians did not like it, they still would attend negotiations sponsored by the United States in spite of it. Occasionally, the U.S. would indicate its displeasure with the construction, stating it was not helpful, but that was as far as the complaint would go. That was, however, before Obama. It was the president, and not the Palestinians, that suddenly made the continued settlement building in East Jerusalem an issue, declaring that negotiations between the parties could not resume before settlement building ended.[2,3,4,5] With this new requirement added by the U.S. president, it was now impossible for the Palestinians to return to their long held position of negotiating without a suspension in Israeli construction in East Jerusalem. In effect, the Palestinians could not allow the American president to be more pro-Palestinian than they were. Thus, from that point forward, the Palestinians, taking their cue from the American president, refused to sit at the negotiating table unless the Israelis adhered to this new requirement. As a result, not only were the positions between the parties widened, no negotiations took place.

Commentators and Middle East observers, who had carefully watched the region for years, were puzzled by the administration's action, with many viewing it as incompetency, instead of diplomacy. Why, they would ask, would anyone create a new requirement for getting the conflicted parties to sit down and talk? Eventually, in an effort to meet the new Obama requirement, a *de facto* suspension of issuing building permits for construction in East Jerusalem suddenly took place, but without a formal order being issued. If asked, the Netanyahu government would deny it. As a result the Palestinians returned to the negotiating table for two months, thereafter, refusing again to come back. As damaging to the peace process as that new Obama requirement had been, it would only be the beginning of policies that would puzzle Middle East observers.

The strange thing about the whole affair was that the new Obama condition was not something to be negotiated in talks between the parties, but something that would prevent talks from even taking place unless agreed to prior to negotiations beginning. If there is another instance of such an approach in the annals of United States diplomacy, it is difficult to find.

****

The Middle East is a powder keg kept away from the fires of radicalism by a handful of key Arab allies of the United States, such as Egypt, Saudi Arabia, and Jordan. Each of these U.S. allies has something in common; they are either threatened by an organization called the Muslim Brotherhood, or some other terrorist organization that is an offshoot such as al-Qaeda, Hamas, Jamma Islamiya, as well as a number of others.[6] Founded in 1928 by an Egyptian school teacher, the Brotherhood grew during the 1930s into a political force to be reckoned with inside Egypt. During the Second World War, it sided with the Nazis against the British, even translating Hitler's derangements catalogued in *Mein Kampf* into Arabic, causing a deepening of hostility toward Western nations.

Carrying on the Brotherhood tradition into 2011, its spiritual guide, Yusuf al-Qaradawi, advises the mutilating of young girls' genitals for the sake of sexual purity. After explaining the good derived from that holy obligation, he usually goes on to explain the benefits of exterminating world Jewry. The Brotherhood's goal is a simple one, a worldwide Islamic caliphate governed by Shariah law where men can kill their daughters should they experience a perceived dishonor. But after years of frontally assaulting their host governments in pursuit of their goals, and suffering the power of state as a consequence, they developed a new tactic, the da'wa. Simply stated, the da'wa, or peaceful outreach, must be employed before conquest can be achieved. As such, the Brotherhood has, in recent years, taken a much more diplomatic approach allowing their offspring, which includes al-Qaeda, to handle the murderous work their ideology commands against all infidels.[7]

There is a weakness, however, that is inherent in governments suppressing the Brotherhood, keeping at bay the forces of radicalism from exploding on the Middle East stage. It is called dictatorship. Simply stated, the populations of these nations, if given the choice, would choose radicalism over the moderate governance imposed on them from many of their nonelected leaders. This is why presidents and prime ministers for decades have taken great care not to rattle the democratic cage of moderate Muslim dictatorships. When considering what might be the result if such an improvident policy is initiated, a look at the years 1978-79 along with President Jimmy Carter and Iran, is helpful.

The Shah of Iran, a staunch ally of the United States and a strong moderating force for peace in the region, was undercut by the American president, who idealistically, but foolishly, moralized on how unfortunate it was that the Iranian people did not have democracy. The ultimate result of Carter's idealism was the overthrow of the Shah, replaced by a murderous regime headed by Ayatollahs dedicated to creating chaos throughout the region. Now, instead of being a moderating force, Iran is seeking nuclear weapons and rockets to deliver them: their target Israel their-stated goal, the killing of every man, woman, and child in the Jewish state.

Within Egypt, under the leadership of President Hosni Mubarak, the Camp David peace accords with Israel continued to be upheld, in spite of popular discontent against them. A Pew Research poll conducted in Egypt between late March and early April 2011 said it all. After polling 1,000 adults, the results indicated that only 34% supported maintaining peace with Israel, while fully 54% supported annulling the treaty. Egypt is a nation that has had peace with Israel for over 30 years. Yet, in spite of that success, the majority appear to prefer a state of conflict with its peaceful neighbor.[8] Therefore, after the revolution that rocked Egypt in early 2011 was finished, deposing the friendly Mubarak and leaving the military in charge, it was no surprise that the men in uniform began aligning with the radical Muslim Brotherhood. Immediately after Mubarak left office, Brotherhood leader Kamal al-Hilbawi flew to Iran for an Islamic unity conference being held there. After the conference, he declared his wish to see Egypt emulate Iran's theocracy.[9] Later, in another example of the Brotherhood's philosophy, after Osama bin Laden was killed by U.S. forces, the Muslim Brotherhood condemned the killing.[10]

In spite of the U.S State Department being well aware of the Brotherhood's history and radical views, President Obama undercut the long-term Egyptian ally, assisting in driving him from power in support of democracy that was almost certain to bring about a radical new order. The results of Obama abandoning the longtime ally were already beginning to be seen by mid 2011. Since the overthrow of the Shah in Iran in 1979, Egypt refused to allow any Iranian warships to transit the Suez Canal, thus greatly restricting Iran's ability to spread its chaos beyond its immediate region. However, since the revolution in Egypt, Iran is once again being allowed to send warships off the coast of Israel, via the Suez Canal. But there is more. Already, the peace treaty between Israel and Egypt, sustained for decades under Mubarak and his predecessor Sadat, is being questioned. In the field of energy, Egypt is under a contract to export natural gas to Israel. After the revolution, however, the gas pipeline leading to Israel was damaged resulting in the cessation of the flow of natural gas from Egypt to Israel. Once it was repaired, however, the government in Cairo refused to resume the flow, breaking its contractual obligation to Israel. In one fell swoop, the progress of presidents dating back to Roosevelt had been reversed.

The other pillar of U.S. support in the troubled region is oil rich Saudi Arabia. After watching the Obama administration in Washington undercut the long term U.S. ally in Egypt, the Saudis became enraged with the president. In a phone conversation reported in the media, its leader, Prince Abdullah, exchanged sharp words with President Obama over his handling of the Egyptian revolution.[11] As another U.S. ally in the region, and one cooperating in the war on terror, the Saudis are critical to U.S. security. The Saudis, realizing Obama would abandon them as well, should unrest erupt in their kingdom, took a step few would have imagined possible only a short time earlier. In a move that clearly begins a shift of even more power away from America in the region, Abdullah began sending emissaries to both China and Russia, seeking enhanced ties with both. Of course, the only way to obtain such an improvement in relations would come directly at the expense of the U.S. By undercutting the two most important U.S. allies in the region, decades of carefully nurtured efforts by American presidents since the 1940s were reversed.[12]

U.S. Secretary of State Hillary Clinton and Defense Secretary Robert Gates attempted to visit the desert kingdom in an effort to smooth things over, but the Saudis would have none of it, refusing to accept either party. That rebuff, unthinkable before Obama, would only be the tip of the Saudi iceberg of trouble. When the revolutionary fever spread from Egypt to neighboring Bahrain, the Saudis quickly sent troops into that country to quell the demonstrations, ignoring U.S. protests as though they had come from some minor nation.[13]

In Tunisia, where the great Arab Revolution began, its relatively moderate leader, Zine al-Abidine Ben Ali a friend of the U.S., fell from power. Here too he is expected to be replaced with a leader approved of by the Muslim Brotherhood. Obama, relatively quick to undercut U.S. allies embroiled in the revolution fever, urging Mubarak to quit in spite of the Egyptian army not being used against the protesters, found it challenging to respond when the revolution spread to a U.S. enemy. In Syria, where the Alawite dictatorship of the Assad regime has been in power for decades, involving itself in the assassination of a neighbor's leader, and aligning with radical Iran, the president was more cautious. Finally, after Assad began using tanks and machine guns to kill hundreds, possibly thousands of his unarmed fellow countrymen, the most Obama could manage was to urge Assad to stop using his army against them. However, he was unable to bring himself to demand Assad's resignation. Oddly, in the case of Syria, virtually any change in the leadership of that country would have been an improvement for the region as well as U.S. influence. Jackson Diehl, writing for *The Washington Post* in an article titled "Why is Obama so tough on Israel and timid on Syria," would note that, "...just twice since the massacres began three months ago" in Syria had Obama said anything about the atrocities. Assad, with the help of Iran, had heavily armed the terrorist organization Hezbollah, an army of 40,000 on Israel's Lebanese border, and as a result, the threat of war on that border with Israel was constant. An end to the Assad regime could have spelled trouble for Hezbollah and reduced radical Iran's influence. Oddly, the president apparently did not find the case for calling on Assad to resign as compelling as the one for Mubarak.

In the Middle East, often the choice is between the lesser of two evils, and so it is in the Israeli-Palestinian dispute. Not long after Israeli Prime Minister Ariel Sharon relinquished control of Gaza to the Palestinians, the area became a base for massive rocket attacks fired from Gaza into Israel. Gaza had originally been turned over to the Palestinian Authority, the only entity on the Palestinian side that Israel would negotiate with. The Palestinian Authority at that time was dominated by Fatah, the strongest political party within Palestinian circles. Not long after the transfer, however, Hamas, a rival of Fatah with most of its support concentrated in Gaza, wrestled control from Fatah in an armed revolt. From that point, Hamas ruled Gaza while Fatah ruled parts of the West Bank. The issue between the two was a simple one: Fatah was not murderous enough for Hamas, even though it too had been killing Israeli men, women, and kids for decades. As Hamas consolidated its control in Gaza, rocket attacks into Israel increased dramatically.

The issue of rocket attacks emanating from Gaza was directly related to the Rafah Crossing, a highway connecting Gaza and Egypt. Essentially, the crossing operated as a weapons sieve allowing large quantities of arms to flow into the hands of Hamas on a regular basis. As a violation of the Camp David Peace Accord between Egypt and Israel, the government in Jerusalem would continually protest to Egypt, their words falling on deaf ears. Finally, after Hamas began fomenting trouble within Egypt itself, the Mubarak government shut the route down, effectively stopping arms shipments flowing into the hands of Hamas. But with the overthrow of Mubarak and the ascension of the Muslim Brotherhood within Egypt, the policy concerning the Rafah Crossing changed. Apparently no longer concerned about radical influences being imported from the Hamas controlled area, Egypt reopened the route. Not long after the reopening, however, the U.S. would persuade the Egyptians to close it again. But the post-revolution Egypt had already shown its new face, one willing to accommodate murderous Hamas, the offspring of the Muslim Brotherhood.

After the reopening of the Rafah Crossing, Mohammed Awad, the

Hamas minister of foreign affairs, expressed his delight at the Egyptian decision that he "highly appreciates the decision by the Egyptian brothers to ease the process of travel at Rafah terminal. This reflects the deep relations between us and Egypt...." Naming the "brothers" as the reason for the reopening of the weapons route, Awad had reason to be pleased. Egypt, apparently now in agreement with that goal, was sending a clear signal to Israel concerning the peace documents signed by its former leader, and hailed across the world as a grand and courageous step for peace in the region. But as ominous as the temporary Rafah opening was to the prospects of peace in the region, it was another development that would have even greater repercussions.[14]

Since Hamas rebelled against Fatah in 2006, the two have had difficult relations. Israel, wishing to deal with the lesser of the two evils, had been negotiating with Fatah. Additionally, the break between Fatah and Hamas had provided some hope that perhaps a moderate might eventually come out of Fatah, someone within Fatah that would lead the Palestinians to live in peaceful coexistence with the Jewish state next door. However, accomplishing what no moderate Muslim nation could, the new Egypt, now under the increasing influence of the Muslim Brotherhood, brokered peace between Fatah and Hamas, creating a new and even more radical front within the Palestinian ranks against Israel.

With Hamas now a partner in the Palestinian Authority, the Obama Administration had a problem. The organization had been labeled a "terrorist" entity for many years, failing to meet three basic requirements before the U.S. and other nations would consider it a legitimate political force and thus qualifying it for U.S. foreign aid. First, it needed to recognize Israel's right to exist, secondly, it needed to agree to respect existing agreements, and third, it needed to renounce terrorism. On all three Hamas was unwilling to compromise.

As a result of not being able to get Hamas to alter its ways, it was the Obama Administration that decided to change.[15]

If you cannot lead a horse to water, then bring the water to the horse. Apparently, not concerned if the Hamas horse will drink the water of Middle East peace, the Obama Administration began lowering the bar established for it to be considered civilized. By creating the façade that Hamas had passed the muster of acceptance, the division within the Palestinian ranks would finally be healed, allowing a united front to be established against Israel. As a result, administration officials began making media appearances where apologies for Hamas were offered. In one such effort, speaking to David Ignatius of *The Washington Post*, they indicated that Hamas, in reconciling with Fatah, had agreed to the terms of a 2009 unity deal worked out by Mubarak, wherein such a unity government would not include Hamas terrorists. Hearing such proclamations being expressed by administration officials in their desperate efforts to rehabilitate the terrorist organization's image, Hamas leader Khaled Mashal, apparently worried the world might actually begin to believe his group was no longer dedicated to killing children, clarified the matter in an interview with *The New York Times*. In the interview, shortly after the deal with Fatah, he made it clear that Hamas did not agree to any moderation of its murderous ways, it was Fatah, he claimed, that changed, adding annexes to the agreement to reflect Hamas positions.[16]

The Obama Administration, continuing its effort to create the best image possible for Hamas, had its supporters go to the media to promote the new line. In one such case, writing in an op-ed in *The Washington Post*, former Obama campaign adviser Robert Malley offered the belief that once a part of the "peace" process, Hamas would obviously "moderate" its positions and behavior. *The New York Times*, probably expressing the ultimate belief within the administration, advised that even if Hamas did not moderate, "Washington needs to press Mr. Netanyahu back to the peace table."[17] The *Times* apparently found it too insignificant to report that it had been Obama's new condition for talks that had prevented negotiations from happening in the first place.

The effort to change the perception that Hamas was a terrorist organization would add new and significant voices in what appeared to be a coordinated effort to help the group's image. Turkish Prime Minister Recip Erdogan and leading Egyptian presidential candidate Amr Moussa did their best to put lipstick on the Hamas pig, denying it was a terrorist group. However, well known for targeting children in its attacks, the pig would keep moving as the cosmetics were being applied. Around the time its image was being worked on by its apologists, Hamas targeted a school bus inside Israel, finding success in murdering 16-year-old Daniel Viflic on his way home from school one day.[18]

Yunis Al-Astal, a cleric and member of Hamas, spoke openly on what many in the organization think. He made it clear that the Jews were, "...brought in droves to Palestine so that the Palestinians – and the Islamic nation behind them will have the honor of annihilating the evil of this gang." But just in case the listener didn't get the message, Al-Astal explained that, "...all the predators, all the birds of prey, all the dangerous reptiles and insects, and all the lethal bacteria are far less dangerous than the Jews."[19]

*　*　*　*　*　*　*

Promising "change" during his 2008 presidential campaign, the new president succeeded in bringing it to the Middle East and especially the alignment of forces arrayed against Israel. No longer was the Jewish state able to find comfort in knowing that the most populous Arab nation in the Middle East, and on its border, was standing strong in its peace treaty with it. Instead, the "change" that occurred brought an old nemesis of the West, the Muslim Brotherhood, out of the shadows and into seats of power in Cairo. Saudi Arabia, the other powerful U.S. ally in the region, seeing the betrayal of a long time U.S. ally in Egypt, would turn to opponents of the U.S., Russia and China, in an effort to find new allies, realigning their foreign policy for the first time since the 1940s. Now, with Hamas joining hands with Fatah, creating a united Palestinian front against Israel, Obama's "change" found its way to the door step of Israel.

Suddenly, as 2011 began with a new and much more dangerous constellation of enemies arrayed against Israel, President Obama made his move. Hindsight is 20-20, allowing observers to understand actions that previously were puzzling. In the case of Obama, the Middle East puzzle he created was confusing at first. Observers of the region had trouble putting in context his move shortly after taking office to create a new condition before negotiations between Israel and the Palestinians could begin, essentially killing them before they started. Then another piece of the puzzle appeared as Obama undercut long time U.S. ally Mubarak as revolutions swept the Middle East, but was much more generous to America's enemy, Syria, as its dictator mowed down protestors by the hundreds. Puzzling yet again, in the case of Egypt, Obama had to know the Muslim Brotherhood was waiting in the wings and with it a catastrophe for Israel and the U.S. Adding another piece to the confusing puzzle was the Fatah-Hamas reconciliation. Why would Fatah be willing to accommodate the extremist Hamas, suddenly mending bridges with it? Didn't it know that the result would be a withdrawal of the significant U.S. support it had been receiving for several years? Strangely, Obama did not change U.S. support for the Palestinian Authority in spite of the unity deal. And why would the administration attempt to make bloody Hamas appear more civilized, even as its leader reassured the world of its commitment to murder?

On May 19, 2011, in a major foreign policy speech, the president would supply the missing piece to his Middle East puzzle, one that would explain his actions which had previously been confusing. After the picture was formed, a disturbing image would emerge. Hannibal's pincer movement was effectively in place with the President of the United States manning one of its flanks.

CHAPTER SEVEN

The Obama Mideast Puzzle

The Israeli jet fighters took off at 7:14 a.m., every last one of them in the entire air force of Israel, with the exception of only twelve that remained behind to protect the nation's air space. Their timing was no accident. Israeli intelligence reports have a habit of being quite detailed, and as such they had revealed a seemingly insignificant fact about the Egyptian Air Force. All of the Egyptian fighter pilots tended to eat breakfast at the same time, but at different air bases. In less than two hours after leaving their bases inside Israel, the Jewish air force struck the Egyptian air force, finding it on the ground and completely destroying it, all 300 planes. After leaving the skies of Egypt, the Israeli strike force proceeded to attack the Jordanian and Syrian Air Forces, here too finding great success. Amazingly, by the end of the first day of fighting, the entire air forces of Egypt and Jordan no longer existed, and in Syria, only half remained. The day was June 5, 1967.[1]

Israel would go on to defeat the combined armies of all three nations on the ground as well. In the blast-furnace conditions of the Sinai desert, Israeli columns of tanks would meet their Egyptian counterparts in classic tank battles, and, with complete supremacy in the air, the Israelites wiped them out. With much the same story playing out on the Syrian and Jordanian fronts, in just six days Israel would score a victory of Biblical proportions against forces that numerically were vastly superior. The spoils would include large spreads of lands from their enemies, including the entire Sinai desert as a new buffer against Egypt, and the Golan Heights from Syria. But it was from Jordan that the real treasure would be taken, the holy city of Jerusalem, sacred to the Jews for thousands of years. The main prize within Jerusalem was the Old City where the ancient Holy of Holies, the Temple of Solomon, had once stood on the Temple Mount. Strangely, in spite of the Temple Mount being holy ground to the Jews, control of it was immediately given back to the Muslim Council, and Jews were barred from conducting prayers there. This was done to avoid an explosion across the Muslim world because Jews were now in control of Muslim sacred grounds.

Although the war would start with a surprise attack on June 5 and last only six days, the rumblings building up to it were long in coming. After Israel's war for independence in 1948, where the surrounding Arab nations attempted to kill the new country by immediately attacking it, war rhetoric and threats continued as the norm in the years that followed. It had been the United Nations that had voted in 1947 for the creation of both a Jewish state and an Arab state in the British protectorate called Palestine. Britain, who gained control of the region after the First World War gave the troubled area to the newly formed United Nations after the Second World War, to distribute as it saw fit. The decision was made by the world body to divide it between the two peoples that constituted the population of Palestine, Jews and Arabs. But the Arabs within Palestine, as well as those in the surrounding area, would have none of it. They attacked the new and peaceful Jewish state and ultimately, as a result of their attack, forfeited the Arab state. Israel would win their nationhood against miraculous odds, and the angry Muslims surrounding them would never forgive the Jews for surviving.[2]

In 1965, Egyptian leader Gamal Nasser, only the second leader of Egypt since disposing the Egyptian monarchy in 1952, made it as clear as possible that Israel must go. In that year he would say, "We shall not enter Palestine with its soil covered in sand; we shall enter with its soil saturated in blood." Shortly after those remarks, he would reiterate, "...we aim at the destruction of the state of Israel. The immediate aim: perfection of Arab military might. The national aim: the eradication of Israel."[3]

After having just suffered through the Holocaust only a few years earlier, the Jews paid attention to such threats. Then on May 15, 1967, Egypt began moving a large number of troops into the Sinai desert, next to the border with Israel. Along Israel's northern front, Syria also began moving troops toward its border with the peaceful Jewish state in clear preparation for war. Then, in an even more ominous sign, Nasser ordered the United Nations peace-keeping force out of the Sinai desert where it had been stationed since 1956, to prevent a war between Egypt and Israel. When the United Nations withdrawal was complete, the Voice of the Arabs radio station read the following Egyptian government statement:

> As of today, there no longer exists an international emergency force to protect Israel. We shall exercise patience no more. We shall not complain any more to the UN about Israel. The sole method we shall apply against Israel is total war, which will result in the extermination of Zionist existence.[4]

From Syria came similar remarks from Defense Minister, Hafez Assad, who acidly announced: "The Syrian army, with its finger on the trigger, is united...I, as a military man, believe that the time has come to enter into a battle of annihilation."

On May 22, in violation of the Convention on the Territorial Sea and Contiguous Zone agreement adopted by the UN in 1958, Egypt closed the Straits of Tiran to all shipping going to or from Israel. The day after the closing, Nasser issued a challenge to Israel, stating, "The Jews threaten to make war. I reply: Welcome! We are ready for war." Then, a few days later he would add, "Our basic objective will be the destruction of Israel. The Arab people want to fight...we will not accept coexistence with Israel...Today the issue is not the establishment of peace between Arab states and Israel...The war with Israel is in effect since 1948."[5]

The Arab forces had good reason to believe they could destroy the small Jewish nation. What made an attack against Israel so attractive to their Muslim enemies was the width of Israel, only nine miles from the Mediterranean to its border with Jordan. Literally, should an Arab armor column drive nine miles from Jordan toward the sea, the nation foretold in the ancient Scriptures would cease to exist.

Then on June 4, apparently unable to resist spilling the blood of the Jews, Iraq joined forces with Egypt, Jordan, and Syria bringing the total Arab forces arrayed against the small Jewish state to 465,000 troops, 2,800 tanks, and 800 aircraft. Fearing that should the vastly superior forces lined up against them strike first, Israel could be destroyed, the order to attack was given. Early on the morning of June 5, the Israeli air force was launched.[6]

* * * * * * *

Having secured large tracts of the Promised Land as a result of the war, Israel would immediately attempt to barter it back to the Arab nations surrounding her in exchange for peace. Considering that those same neighbors had built up troops on the border with Israel as they voiced intentions to wipe the Jewish state out of existence, the offer was considered by most as generous. Her Arab neighbors, however, soundly rejected the offer, assuring the world that the fight was not over. They would make good on that threat six years later. On the Jewish religious holiday of Yom Kippur, Egypt and Syria launched a new war, attempting to take back the lands lost in 1967, and ultimately hoping to drive the Jews, every man, woman, and child into the sea. Preferring war to a peaceful settlement of the conflict, their forces would achieve strategic surprise, driving deep into the Sinai and Golan Heights in the beginning of the war. But Israel, fighting for its life, would soon turn the tide on them, eventually threatening the capitals of both nations.

The 1973 Yom Kippur War, as it would be called, represented the third time since its rebirth that Israel was attacked by her Arab neighbors, or, as was the case in 1967, was about to be. The first attack came in 1948, the day after the state of Israel was declared, reborn after almost two thousand years just as the ancient Hebrew Scriptures promised. The next two wars came in 1967, and finally the 1973 Yom Kippur War where both Syria and Egypt launched a surprise attack to retake the lands it lost to the small and outnumbered Jews only a few years earlier. Interestingly, Jordan did not participate in that war. One of the reasons was that Israel controlled the West Bank since its 1967 victory, providing its military with the advantage of strategic depth that Jordan chose not to test. Eventually, Israel returned the Sinai desert to Egypt, in return for peace and the demilitarization of the area. In fact, the demilitarization of the Sinai represented the continuation of protective depth on the Egyptian front with Israel getting a historic peace agreement thrown in the deal.

It had been former Egyptian President Anwar Sadat, seizing the historic moment, who agreed to the deal in 1978. In spite of enormous pressure from Muslims across the world, the stately leader marched to his own tune, one of peace instead of blood. But it was not a tune recognized by many in his country, ultimately costing the courageous Egyptian his life. Today after over 30 years of peace between the former enemies, the grand peace accords are in jeopardy as the winds of "revolution" blow across the Middle East. With Mubarak gone, the ascension of the Muslim Brotherhood has begun, no longer suppressed by the friendly dictator. Ironically, it is once again that same Muslim Brotherhood that threatens the agreement. But this time its threat doesn't come from the dark shadows where assassins plot sinister schemes, but from the halls of power. This single fact presents an unfortunate Middle East development, one quite unfriendly to peace in the region and to the future of Israel. But it also provides another piece to a new Middle East puzzle, one developing since the election of Obama.

* * * * * * *

In the first major foreign policy speech of his presidency, Obama chose Cairo as the location for the much anticipated talk. New American presidents telegraph great significance to the world of foreign policy watchers by what is accentuated early in their administration, the location of their first major foreign policy speech being viewed as quite significant, leaving an indelible mark that the area of the world chosen will be the new administration's focus. Details are carefully watched as well for any sign that the 900-pound world gorilla might be making a change in direction. Slight nuances of who is invited and who is not are watched with care indicating, essentially, who will be in favor during the new administration and who will not. It was here that the first Mideast policy confusion began to ring out from the new president.

In the audience would be individuals of influence throughout Egypt. Included in that number would also be ten members of the Muslim Brotherhood. This raised the eyebrows of Arab moderates in the region, wondering if the new president was signaling a shift in U.S. policy and for many, a potentially ominous one. As a political force that spawned numerous terrorist organizations since its founding in 1928, the Brotherhood's presence was disconcerting. To Arabs allied with the United States and dedicated to suppressing radical forces in the region, it would be a first sign, a foretaste of a bitter cup. But the invitation to the group's members also represented a political slap in the face to the long time U.S. ally, Egyptian leader Hosni Mubarak, the host of the event. It was comparable to being invited to a good friend's intimate dinner party, and bringing his ex-wife along, when their bitter divorce isn't quite finished. None-the-less, the Brotherhood was there.

As word spread that the Brotherhood was invited, Rep. Pete Hoekstra, ranking Republican on the House intelligence committee, echoed what many were thinking, "What kind of signal are we sending?"[7] Indeed, it was a strange signal. As reported in the media at the time of the Cairo speech, one of the Brotherhood's goals is the establishment of an Islamic state. Such a state would, undoubtedly, be naturally aligned with Iran, another Islamic state. And with another Iran in the region, this time bordering Israel, the prospects for peace would virtually disappear.

Since the organization is officially banned within Egypt, its candidates run for parliament as independents. For those inside Egypt that fear the Brotherhood's rise would lead to an Islamic state similar to Iran, all means available to suppress them is considered fair. Because the organization has considerable sway within the country, Mubarak, like his predecessors before him had, frequently used the Egyptian military to suppress them. This resulted in the group changing its tactics, causing it to openly renounce the use of violence. But its offspring would do more than enough killing to make up for it.

After the assassination of Sadat in 1981, a subsequent investigation found that the Brotherhood offshoot, Al Gamaa al-Islamiyya had been the main instigator. The stated reason for killing Sadat was his having made peace with Israel. Viewed as an apostate, he was condemned to death by the Muslim Brotherhood offspring. Among the group's leaders was Ayman al-Zawahiri, who was sentenced to three years in prison for his part in the infamous act. Later, al-Zawahiri would become the number one man of al-Qaeda after bin Laden was killed.[8]

In a February 2011 *National Review* article looking at the Brotherhood, Andrew McCarthy a terrorism expert, would put it this way:

> This is the Muslim Brotherhood whose motto brays that the Koran is its law and jihad is its way. The MB whose Palestinian branch, the terrorist organization Hamas, was created for the specific purpose of destroying Israel—the goal of its charter says it is a religious obligation. It is the organization dedicated to the establishment of Islamicized societies and, ultimately, a global caliphate. It is an organization whose leadership says al-Qaeda's emir, Osama bin Laden, is an honorable jihad warrior who was "close to Allah on high" in "resisting the occupation."[9]

Again, in the *National Review* article, McCarthy quotes the Muslim Brotherhood's "Supreme Guide," Muhammad Badi, who expressed his hope for a "jihadi generation that pursues death, just as the enemies pursue life." Adding further clarity to the Brotherhood and its intentions, senior Brotherhood member Kamal al-Halbavi expressed what many in the organization were hoping would come out of the revolution in Egypt, a government, "...like the Iranian government, and a good president like Mr. Ahmadinejad."[10] Of course, that is the same Iranian leader that is feverishly seeking nuclear weapons and rockets to deliver them to fulfill his often stated goal of annihilating Israel.

However, as the 2011 revolution inside Egypt raged, the military in that country stood to the side considering what actions, if any, to take in support of Mubarak. Their dilemma was a simple one. Should they stand with the embattled Mubarak, waiting out the protestors, or begin turning away from him? As a military almost completely dependent on the U.S. for its weapons and training, the eyes of its leading officers looked West to Washington for a sign of how strongly America would stand with its ally. Should the U.S. waver in its support as the critical moment for Mubarak arrived, it would bode ill for the West's friend and very good for the Muslim Brotherhood. On the other hand, a clear commitment that the United States would stand behind Mubarak, perhaps supporting a transition of power to another military man, and the Brotherhood would be checkmated. But Mubarak would resign the day after Obama appeared on TV and rebuked him. The Egyptian military, sensing the shift in U.S. support away from Mubarak, saw what side to take. The rebuke would be the final straw for the embattled American ally.[11]

In the U.S., House Republican chair of the Foreign Affairs Committee, Ileana Ros-Lehtinen would sum up the concerns of many following Mubarak's resignation stating:

> We must also urge the unequivocal rejection of any involvement by the Muslim Brotherhood and other extremists who may seek to exploit and hijack these events to gain power, oppress the Egyptian people, and do great harm to Egypt's relationship with the United States, Israel and other free nations..."[12]

But the main concern in any democratic election within Egypt was the Brotherhood. Since it was the most politically organized group in the nation, and popular for its strong Islamist and grass roots approach, it was a heavy favorite in any election. Throughout the world, free and fair elections usually mean a moderate government, except within the Middle East. As an area of the world where radicalism has widespread support within the ranks of the common man, the greatest threat to the West would, strangely, come from democracy. For example, in the case of Iran, after its first election the friendly Shah was replaced with a radically anti-western Islamic republic. In Iraq after Saddam Hussein was removed, free elections have produced a government increasingly friendly to Iran, instead of the previous one that had been a counter-weight to the ambitions of the mullahs in Tehran. In Tunisia, where the great Arab revolution began, the Muslim Brotherhood is favored to win their first free election.

After the revolution in Egypt was over and it became apparent that the Brotherhood would, indeed, be the political force to be reckoned with, the Obama administration's James Clapper, U.S. Director of National Intelligence, would provide extraordinary testimony before the House Intelligence Committee. In a surreal moment for those familiar with the Brotherhood, he would state before the committee that:

> The term 'Muslim Brotherhood'...is largely an umbrella term for a variety of movements, in the case of Egypt, a very heterogeneous group, largely secular, which has eschewed violence and has decried Al Qaeda as a perversion of Islam...there is no overarching agenda, particularly in the pursuit of violence...[13]

Not long after Clapper delivered his statement, the Brotherhood would make a mockery of his testimony, issuing a statement condemning the U.S. killing of Osama bin Laden. After hearing of Clapper's testimony, John Bolton, former U.S. Ambassador to the United Nations, would voice that the comments were, "...perhaps the stupidest statement made by any administration in U.S. international history." Clapper would retract the "secular" part of his statement, leaving the remaining part as his opinion.[14]

Present in the Clapper incident was another puzzling Obama Middle East event, leading to the most natural of questions: Why would an administration official as significant as the U.S. Director of National Intelligence make such a statement? The entire effort appeared to be an attempt to rehabilitate the image of the Brotherhood, from the reality of the mother of numerous Muslim terrorist organizations, to a reasonable, freedom-loving organization that was badly misunderstood. Why?

Again, signals sent by the President of the United States are watched with care in the Middle East, the players carefully maneuvering to avoid being stepped on by the biggest gorilla in the room. By making statements and taking actions that confer a form of legitimacy on the Brotherhood, its chances of rising to power increased. No longer treated as a danger by the world's only superpower, the Brotherhood's leaders would point this out as they sought support from otherwise moderate forces within the country. No doubt that same message was not lost on the Egyptian military as well.

The revolution in Egypt had the quality of essentially being a leaderless revolt with masses of individuals going out into the streets, beckoned by Facebook and Twitter. Thus, without a clear leader who the voters could express approval upon in the first election, the results will come down to the best organized faction in the country. That leaves the Muslim Brotherhood. As the Egyptian revolution was raging, the *Los Angeles Times* noted something about the administration's approach to the group that, even to them, appeared surprising. Referring to the Muslim Brotherhood:

> The organization must reject violence and recognize democratic goals if the U.S. is to be comfortable with it taking part in the government, the White House said. <u>But by even setting conditions for the involvement of such non-secular groups, the administration took a surprise step in the midst of the crisis...</u>"
> (emphasis added)

Indeed, the administration had taken a surprising step, signaling to the world, but more importantly, to the Egyptian military, its willingness to accommodate the Muslim Brotherhood. The White House, already aware that the Brotherhood had ceased directly engaging in violent activities allowing the various terrorist organizations spawned from it to fulfill that jihad obligation, could later claim it was a peaceful organization. All the while, having spoken such words of comfort and support for the Brotherhood, the White House in the same breath was effectively driving nails into the coffin of America's Egyptian friend and bulwark against radical Islam.

* * * * * * *

The beginning of a puzzle is the most difficult part. There are so many pieces to be placed somewhere, and yet no scant corner of the ultimate picture to help guide the puzzle maker. But eventually a piece here and there begin fitting, a sense of the ultimate picture starts coming into focus. Now the following pieces of an unusual Middle East puzzle, a new one never before designed by an American president, has begun to form. Here are the pieces so far.

PUZZLE PIECE #1

Bringing the Muslim Brotherhood out of the Shadows

Obama signals to the world that it will be the Middle East where his main foreign policy efforts would be devoted, heading to Cairo to deliver his first major foreign policy speech. Surprisingly, the Muslim Brotherhood is invited and will be in the audience at Cairo University. It is a slap in the face of long time U.S. ally Hosni Mubarak and lends credibility to the radical group.

PUZZLE PIECE #2

Spiking Israeli-Palestinian Negotiations

Master U.S. diplomat George Mitchell is undercut in his efforts to narrow the differences between the Israelis and Palestinians, with negotiations prevented by a new requirement being added as a prerequisite before they can begin. But it is Obama, not the Palestinians, that adds the condition that all construction by Israel in East Jerusalem must end. It then becomes the Palestinians' new requirement ending any chance for negotiations.

PUZZLE PIECE #3

Undercutting Mubarak and Opening the Door of Power to the Muslim Brotherhood

The Obama Administration undercut long term U.S. friend and ally Hosni Mubarak in his time of need. To many observers of the region, there is only one realistic outcome to this action, the ascendency of the Muslim Brotherhood to power.

PUZZLE PIECE #4

Rehabilitating the Muslim Brotherhood's Image

Claiming the Muslim Brotherhood had changed its evil ways, the Obama Administration would have one of their leading security men make claims to Congress that were not only fictitious, but ridiculous. Why would any U.S. administration attempt to improve the image of the organization that mothered both Hamas and al-Qaeda?

PUZZLE PIECE #5

Alienating Saudi Arabia

By undercutting the moderate Mubarak regime in Egypt, Saudi Arabia now feels threatened. This is an obvious outgrowth of Obama's actions against Mubarak.

PUZZLE PIECE # 6

Tacitly supporting Assad in his time of trouble

It was one of the most puzzling foreign policy decisions in years, especially when considered in the light of Obama's actions during the Egyptian revolution. As an enemy of America and Israel, Assad, leader of Syria, was mowing down protestors by the hundreds with machine guns and tanks, while Obama refused to call for his resignation.

PUZZLE PIECE #7

Fatah-Hamas Deal & No Repercussions

After Fatah and Hamas form a unity government, Obama does not withdraw financial aid from the Palestinian Authority.

But as disturbing as these developments have been since the new president took office in January 2009, it would take the events unfolding in 2011 to supply the remaining puzzle pieces for the picture to finally form. As the year began, so did a move toward statehood for the Palestinians within the land promised by God to the Israelis.

CHAPTER EIGHT

The Paradox of Duplicity

I n October 2010, the Egyptian foreign minister, Ahmed Abdoul Gheit, provided a glimpse into the immediate future of the Middle East. Arriving for an Arab meeting being held in Brussels, he threatened that if Israel continued building settlements in the West Bank, "...the Arab League will study some other options such as going to the United Nations and ask for recognition of the Palestinian state."[1] He would soon prove to be a prophet. As 2011 began the Palestinian Authority, the ruling entity for the Palestinian Arabs, began a drive for the declaration of statehood by the world body, the same United Nations that had offered the Arabs of Palestine statehood in 1947, alongside a state for the Jews. At that time, however, instead of embracing the idea, they and the Arab nations surrounding Israel attacked in the hope of stopping its rebirth, desiring to take all of the land for themselves. Ultimately, the Arabs lost their fight to kill the new state of Israel, and after the smoke cleared from that war, Israel, Egypt, and Jordan would divide the lands previously meant for a new Arab state. From that time forward from the Arab perspective, destroying the Jewish state became a cause of religious conviction, cleansing the region of Jews in the name of Allah. Now, several decades later and after having fared badly in their efforts against the vastly outnumbered Jews, the Arabs would move to add more nations to their cause by seeking U.N. recognition of a Palestinian state.

The timing for such a move appeared right. With Israel's great friend the United States, weakened in the region by two wars, and a new leader in the White House that appeared more than willing to see the Arab side of things, it could be the best time to take such a step, before circumstances might change again. However, the repercussions for Israel of such a move could be disastrous. As Michael Sfard, an Israeli lawyer in the fields of human rights and military matters noted, once a Palestinian state is admitted to the UN, it suddenly will have various legal options at its disposal that at present do not exist. For over 44 years Israel has been able to utilize its own Supreme Court to review its actions in Judea and Samaria. That will change once the nation of Palestine is declared. Instead of Israeli actions within the Arab populated areas being essentially an internal Israeli matter, they will suddenly attain a distinct international quality. But that is not from where the biggest threat comes.[2]

The biggest threat comes from the ability of the nation of Palestine to engage internationally. As Sfard noted,

> The significance of accepting Palestine as a member of the U.N. is that the new member will be sovereign to sign international treaties, to join international agreements and to receive the jurisdictional authority of international tribunals over what happens in the territory.[3]

After a United Nations vote establishing the nation of Palestine, the new member could, according to international law, demand the removal of all Israeli military forces as well as any Israeli settlements within the borders of the newly established state. Those borders would be the ones in effect the day before the 1967 Six-Day War, the ones that were so tempting for Israel's enemies in fulfilling their hopes of annihilating the "Jewish entity." With almost 500,000 Israeli citizens now within those potential Palestinian borders, the problem is obvious. Unless the above conditions were met, Israel would be occupying a fellow member of the United Nations, with the option of U.N. military action available against the occupier. Those possibilities represent the greatest threat against the land promised in the ancient Hebrew Scriptures since the rebirth of the nation.

As 2011 progressed and, one by one, nations across the world indicated their intention to vote yes for statehood along the dangerous 1967 lines as the new border, Israel's prime minister began the fight of his life, and that of his nation. Those same borders had been referred to by the late Israeli Labor leader Abba Eban as the "Auschwitz Borders," named after the infamous Nazi death camp that exterminated hundreds of thousands of Jews during the Second World War. In April 2011 former U.S. ambassador to Israel, Martin Indyk, predicted that if no changes are made in the peace effort leading up to September, the U.N. will declare a Palestinian state.

In Europe, often a place of support for Israel in a world of opposition, Netanyahu began visiting both Britain and France, hoping to persuade them not to vote yes when the statehood issue comes up before the United Nations. But the signs were not encouraging. Palestinian president Mahmoud Abbas, meeting with French president Nicolas Sarkozy in early May returned home gleeful. Hearing from Sarkozy that "France will face up to its responsibilities on recognition of a Palestinian state," the French leader added, "the idea that there is still plenty of time is dangerous. Things have to be brought to a conclusion..."[5]

Abbas received much the same response in Britain during his trip. Then, in an interview with *France24*, he would brag, "You notice that a certain number of European countries have recently sent additional delegations and official representatives to the Palestinian territories. From our side, we are already treating them like ambassadors."[6]

While in Britain, Netanyahu would be treated to a lecture indicating, ultimately, what the English would do when the vote comes up in the General Assembly. According to an unnamed British diplomatic source:

> Britain's clear and absolute preference is for a negotiation to take place by Israel and the Palestinians which leads to a two-state solution which everyone endorses. But at this point we're not ruling anything out. The more Israel engages seriously in a meaningful peace process, the less likely it is that the question of unilateral declaration would arise.[7]

But this is where the impact of Obama's actions early in his administration now came back to haunt the Israelis. By adding the new requirement that Israel must cease construction in East Jerusalem before negotiations could take place, he had effectively killed the process. In spite of having done this, he would implore the sides to begin negotiations. Indeed, under previous Israeli administrations, Israel had negotiated away control over large tracts of the ancient Promised Land, in Judea and Samaria as well as all of Gaza. From the standpoint of those working to remove the restored lands from Israel, there had been significant success, however, met with the strange "coincidences" of disasters. Now with the British and other European nations urging negotiations that the Obama administration's new condition killed, Israel found itself against a wall, pushed there by its friend, the United States. As former Israeli Mossad chief Efraim Halevy would say, Israel's "maneuvering space is growing narrower." And indeed it had, finding itself in an effective diplomatic "pincer movement" similar to the one Hannibal had used against the Romans some two thousand years earlier.

Already on Israel's border with Syria events began unfolding that appeared to be a harbinger of the impact a Palestinian state declared along the lines of the 1967 border would have. Large numbers of Palestinians began coming across the Golan Heights, with the assistance of the Syrian government, attempting to enter Israel. Member of the Knesset commit-tee chairman Shaul Mofaz warned that such clashes should be expected once the vote is taken in September, adding that the "changes here are tectonic...a precursor to the September events, which could come in waves against Israel's population."[8]

* * * * * * *

In August 2009, only seven months after Obama took office, Pal-estinian Authority (PA) Prime Minister Salam Fayyad made a strange statement. Usually, statements originating from the PA concerning their hopes for a state of their own would be in the context of demanding it as soon as possible. It would also be the norm for the PA to demand more Israeli concessions in negotiations to achieve such a state. However, that August, something changed. In speaking to the *Times of London*, Fayyad would insist that the Palestinian Authority would establish a "de facto" state within the next two years, regardless of how peace talks go. Stating to the reporter that:

> We have decided to be proactive, to expedite the end of the occupation by working very hard to build positive facts on the ground, consistent with having our state emerge as a fact that cannot be ignored...This is our agenda, and we want to pursue it doggedly."[9]

Then, laying out a clear plan, he went on to provide significant de-tails of what would happen over the next two years to get ready for this "de facto" state he was so certain would become a reality. It would include security forces, public services, and a thriving economy. Included in the 65-page plan was a roadmap to erecting institutions and infrastructure, all of which he assured would be ready within two years.[10]

What was most interesting about his statement was how he stressed that the state would be a "de facto" one, essentially not one negotiated with the Israelis. That in itself was a little strange, as the success from sitting down and talking had been significant, over time. But now, for reasons he did not divulge at the time, he envisioned a "de facto" state, one created not from negotiations with the Israelis, but coming from another source.

Amazingly, by April 2011, only five months before the United Nations vote on statehood, a U.N. committee would visit the Palestinian Authority, issuing a report titled, "Palestinian State-Building: A Decisive Period." Coincidentally, just in time for the upcoming statehood vote at the U.N., the report would conclude that, in the six areas where the U.N. is most involved, governmental functions are now sufficient for a functioning Palestinian government of a state. The report then went to a committee in Brussels to receive its stamp of approval.

As reported by the U.N. News Services concerning that meeting:

> ...is the last expected gathering of the committee before the September 2011 target date for completion of institutional readiness for statehood set by the Palestinian Authority and supported by the diplomatic grouping known as the Quartet – which comprises the UN, European Union, Russia and the United States.[11]

Indeed, the Quartet led by the United States and its president were ultimately behind the effort. Without such a powerful group, the Palestinian effort would be dead-on-arrival at the United Nations. As the September U.N. vote approached, everything just happened to be falling into place.

At this point some reflection is necessary. Unless one truly believes in fantastic coincidences, one of two options remains to explain the Fayyad prediction. Either Fayyad is a prophet, able to see into the future, or something much larger had been at play since early in the Obama Administration. How could so insignificant a figure on the world stage, Fayyad, know fully two years before it would happen that the world would back him for a statehood bid before the United Nations and that the necessary institutions required for statehood would be approved by the U.N. just in time for the vote? He couldn't, is the short answer. Some world figure of great power would have had to inform him how it would all play out.

* * * * * * *

On May 19, 2011, President Obama clarified to the world, including his stunned Jewish supporters, his vision of "peace" between the Israelis and Palestinians in a speech that the president of the Arab League could have given. Speaking the day before Israeli Prime Minister Netanyahu was to arrive in Washington to meet with him, the president's speech appeared to be an ambush of the Israeli leader. Taking a position that no American president had ever before, the president laid out a plan that sounded eerily similar to that which would be voted on at the U.N. later in the year. Now having become official policy of the U.S. government, the President of the United States explained to the Israelis the benefits of returning to the "Auschwitz Borders," promised by presidents since 1967 that the U.S. would never require Israel to do. Obama, reversing what presidents since Nixon had held sacrosanct, went on to provide the gory details.[13]

The president went on to explain that Israel needed to agree to return to the indefensible borders of 1967 as a condition for negotiations to begin, not as a settlement, but for negotiations to simply begin. That in itself was staggering, sounding like an opening line to a play written and directed by the late Palestinian leader Yasser Arafat. The result of returning to those borders would be an Israel that was nine miles wide at its center. Should the new Palestinian state align with the likes of the Muslim Brotherhood in Egypt, which was already beginning to happen, and build a military designed for a quick strike against Israel, the Arab goal of a "momentous massacre" would finally be achieved against their hated enemy, the Jews. The threat represented by the "Auschwitz Borders" would represent a drastic altering of Israel's military picture, with a new enemy state within nine miles of dividing it in two in a future conflict. Then with the Muslim Brotherhood replacing the friendly Mubarak on Israel's other flank, the small Jewish state would be ripe for destruction. Added to this mix on the Lebanese border was Hezbollah, also dedicated to the destruction of Israel and having amassed over 40 thousand well armed and trained fighters at that border ready to attack from that flank. Militarily, diplomatically, and psychologically, Israel was enveloped in an effective, even brilliant "pincer movement."

But the president wasn't finished explaining his vision for peace. He did not state his clear opposition to the Palestinian notion of the "right of return" which would mean that millions of Arabs would be allowed to enter and live in Israel, becoming citizens. Due to their much higher birth rates, they would eventually destroy Israel from within by outnumbering them. One would have thought that if the president was offering the Palestinians the 1967 borders, that something like the "right of return" on their part should have to be given up in a standard quid pro quo, but none was indicated in the president's speech.[14]

There was a statement in the president's speech, actually several that surprised the listener, but two in particular stood out. The first was his call for Israel to return to the 1967 indefensible borders. The second was when he called for the new Palestinian state to be "contiguous," essentially with no part of Israel dividing it. That "contiguous" statement meant that Gaza would have to be connected to Judea and Samaria so that the Palestinians could travel the length of their new nation without passing through any part of Israel. But there was an obvious problem achieving that. With a part of Israel placed in between the two Palestinian areas, Israel would have to be divided in two to accomplish the president's goal. What the president was saying is that after 43 years of building infrastructure and homes in an uncontested part of Israel, it would now have to be given up so the Palestinians would not have to suffer having a divided country. Obviously, the president found that dividing Israel was acceptable.[15] Essentially, the president effectively was coming out in his speech for Israel to be bisected so that the new Palestinian state would not have to be, and he was also sending another clear message. Since the land necessary to create a contiguous Palestinian state was not under the rule of either Jordan or Egypt prior to the 1967 war, what he was really asking from Israel was an admission that none of the land it held was secure from being taken away, essentially delegitimizing Israel's existence. Referring to Obama's speech, Glenn Kessler, of *The Washington Post*, would observe, "...it represents a significant shift in U.S. policy, and it is certainly a change for the Obama administration."

But there were more terms to be delivered to the stunned Israelis, who, perhaps, were beginning to feel a bit like the Czechs did in 1938. After giving away control of Gaza in 2005 in an effort to bring peace to the area, Israel experienced a dramatic increase in rocket attacks originating there. The result was barrage after barrage of rocket attacks aimed at peaceful, uncontested Israeli towns just over the border from Gaza. Initially wary of handing over Gaza to those sworn to Israel's destruction, Israeli leader Ariel Sharon was convinced that it was a good idea by a letter of commitment provided by then president George W. Bush. Bush, carrying on a tradition of giving assurances to an American ally that he assumed future presidents would honor, indicated in the letter that by giving up Gaza, in the name of "peace," the United States would not ask Israel to return to the 1967 lines. Also included in the letter were the assurances that large settlement blocks located in the West Bank would be allowed to remain under Israeli control in any agreement, and that the U.S. would oppose the "right of return" that would effectively end Israel as a Jewish state.[16]

Letters given by their predecessors are traditionally respected by presidents, knowing that by respecting previous presidential commitments they infer the same power. As such, both friend and foe understand they can rely upon these letters of understanding to be upheld by future presidents. Obama, again breaking with a host of presidents before him, ignored that U.S. commitment in his speech. By coming out in favor of the "1967 lines with mutually agreed swaps," Obama reversed Bush's commitment used to cede control of Gaza to the Palestinians, viewed at the time as a victory for the "land for peace" crowd. Also, based on Obama's concept of "mutually agreed swaps," whatever Israeli settlements the new Palestinian state did not agree to, would have to be removed. Since they would never agree to allowing Israel to retain any of the settlements within the 1967 borders, Obama's position would effectively result in Israel having to move over 500,000 citizens. How likely was it that the Palestinians would agree to Obama's "swaps?" Since 2000, the Palestinians had been offered three deals with a variation on the 1967 lines including significant swaps, allowing the Israelis to retain their settlements and a defensible border. All were rejected.[17] No doubt those within the administration that opposed the dramatic shift in U.S. Middle East policy against Israel had pointed this fact out to the president. But obviously unmoved by their arguments, it became the new U.S. policy.

During the years preceding the Second World War, Britain, the world's only superpower at the time, in an effort to appease Hitler forced Czechoslovakia to cede a portion of its country to Germany, in the name of "peace." The result was an indefensible border and masses of displaced Czechs. Within a month the Czech Republic ceased to exist, unable to defend itself. That effort on the part of the British leader at the time, Neville Chamberlain, appeared to be the result of his being naïve as to the true nature of the threat Germany presented. His betrayal of a British ally happened in a moment of weakness, as he desperately tried to defuse a looming war. But in the case of Obama, there appears to have been a plodding method to his actions, the kind that belies unseen motives within a person, different from those displayed openly. The president's May 19 speech was enlightening, revealing with clarity for the first time an overt policy, one that had been practiced under the radar for the first two years of his administration. But the timing of it being brought to the surface appears to have been forced by another event.

In mid April 2011, Israeli Prime Minister Netanyahu was invited to address Congress, the speech scheduled for mid-May. In his speech, he was expected to unveil the most generous and aggressive peace proposal yet, one that would place enormous pressure on the Palestinians to return to the negotiating table. After presenting such an offer, should the Palestinians then refuse to reciprocate the onus would be on them, negatively impacting their bid for a declaration of statehood within the United Nations. If a number of the U.N. members ready to vote yes for a new state realized that the Israelis were making grand efforts to resolve the dispute, but it was the Palestinians that were not cooperating, then the votes might not be there in September at the U.N., especially within the European block of votes.

Obama, knowing that Netanyahu would soon be coming, suddenly announced his intention to make his speech on the eve of the Israeli leader's visit. Jackson Diehl, writing for *The Washington Post*, would observe Obama's actions as, "...arguably the most high-handed presidential act in U.S.-Israeli relations since the Eisenhower administration." The obvious motive on the part of Obama was to present his plan first. But that raises the question of why he didn't first want to see how far the Israeli leader was willing to go and see if the dispute could be bridged. That would be the approach used by most diplomats in a dispute. But instead Obama chose to undercut the Israeli effort, delivering a speech that destroyed any chance for Netanyahu to even present his plan in a viable setting. The president's speech placed a final nail in the coffin of negotiations.

Harvard Law professor and Obama supporter Alan Dershowitz, puzzled by Obama's approach, would proclaim after the speech on national TV, "I think it is a terrible tragedy of how he's handled this process" adding that Obama's position "hurt the peace process gravely." Then, referring back to the first time Obama took a step that effectively prevented negotiations by adding a new condition to the mix, Dershowitz would exclaim, "He made the same mistake again in this speech." Dershowitz saw no duplicity in Obama's actions, only incompentency.[18]

Something else took place that was puzzling, and it happened just prior to the president's big Middle East speech of May 19. Top U.S. Middle East "negotiator" George Mitchell, respected as a master diplomat across the world for having found a way to bring peace to Northern Ireland, resigned only days before Obama delivered his speech. The resignation was a surprise. Why would the U.S. point man for the Middle East resign prior to his region of responsibility taking center stage in both the U.S. and at the U.N.? The answer is very simple. As a negotiator of peace settlements, he was no longer needed. He was no longer needed because he obviously had become aware of the new Obama approach to the Middle East, and realized that it would be the final blow against negotiations for years to come. His resignation letter to the president was dated April 6, fully five weeks before it was announced by the administration. Therefore, it must have been in early April that Obama began to unveil the new foreign policy to his advisors for the Middle East, the one presented in his speech several weeks later. It is likely that as Mitchell heard his intentions, the resignation letter was presented. This is speculative, but logical. Mitchell had been negotiating the Middle East for Clinton, Bush and then Obama. Are we to suppose that it is just a coincidence his career would suddenly end only days before Obama delivered a policy speech that ended any chance for negotiations? It is much more likely that it was the fact that there would no longer be any chance for negotiations because of Obama's new Middle East policy that caused his resignation. But why wait five weeks before announcing it? The most logical reason for waiting would be that Mitchell was using his letter as a Sword of Damocles so the president would understand how serious he was. But as the president's speech would prove, it would be to no avail. This, too, is speculative, but again, it is logical. Why else would his resignation not be reported until five weeks later? If it had been held until after the president's speech, then the case could be made that it was held so as not to be disruptive to the president's new approach. But that did not happen. It was released only days *before* the speech. That action could not have pleased the president, inferring disunity within his foreign policy ranks just prior to his big speech that would reverse United States policy toward Israel. But obviously from Mitchell's perspective, it was important to him that it be released *before* the speech, effectively distancing him from what the president was about to do.[19]

In April, fully a month before the president's speech announcing his new Middle East policy, the *Los Angeles Times* reported that the Quartet would recognize a Palestinian state if negotiations did not succeed. Of course, negotiations would first have to take place. In palpable irony, after the Quartet indicated this approach, its leader, Obama, killed any chance of those negotiations taking place with his big speech. Then, after the speech that killed any chance for negotiations was delivered, the group of four strongly endorsed the president's new approach.[20][21]

* * * * * * *

A puzzle exists because its creator intends for a picture to be hidden in the pieces, causing casual onlookers to see only its disparate parts with no ability to form a complete picture. Those disparate parts in their own right will often cause concern, but without the other parts fitted together next to them, the stir is usually minimal. In the case of President Obama's

Middle East approach, it is now obvious why it has been constructed more like a puzzle than a policy. As is usually the case when the work of pulling together a puzzle begins, it eventually comes to an end, producing the reward of a complete picture. After the president's speech on May 19, the final piece of the puzzle has found its place, forming a picture of Obama's Middle East agenda.

Based on available facts, this is what appears to have been taking place since the election of Barack Obama. Sometime in 2009, the president got word to the Palestinians that he would accomplish what they and their Arab allies had been unable to for decades, the creation of a Palestinian state along the 1967 lines. He further must have indicated the time frame associated with the effort as two years. Fayyad, the Palestinian Prime Minister would telegraph this to the world in his sudden announcement in August 2009 that a "de facto" Palestinian state would exist in two years. Since there is only one person on Earth that could possibly accomplish such a thing, that being the president of the United States, it had to be Obama that relayed this to him in private, unable to share his plan with the likes of George Mitchell who believed in negotiations. Fayyad's use of the word "de facto" would provide another hint as to how the state would come about, not through a negotiated settlement, but through other means. That too would prove to be prophetic. Two years later, just as the Palestinian leader had indicated, a "de facto" state would be voted on in the United Nations along the 1967 lines. The time frame of "two years" was a significant clue offered by Fayyad as well. Why "two years?" If it extended much beyond that, the U.S. presidential campaign season would be in full swing, thus tying the hands of Obama. Why not in one year? Because it did not allow enough time for the facade that negotiations had failed, nor would the United Nations have had enough time to certify that the Palestinian Authority had established all of the institutions necessary for a state.

Next, Obama had to stop negotiations from taking place, otherwise that would hinder a United Nations vote; how could they vote as negotiations were taking place? Since too many members would be hesitant to do anything that might interfere with a negotiated settlement between the parties, the act of negotiating would kill the Palestinian U.N. statehood effort. Additionally, the longer the parties went without negotiating, the more the stage would be set to be able to say "something had to be done," since the parties were not even talking. Unable to tell the statesman Mitchell of his plan, Obama would have to create a condition for negotiations to begin that the Israelis would never agree to. Not a condition to be negotiated, but a condition for talks to take place. Had it been a condition to be discussed, then talks would have taken place, thus impacting a U.N. vote. But because it was a condition for negotiations to take place, the talks were killed, just as would be necessary to ultimately force it to the United Nations. This he did early in his administration, insuring negotiations would be spiked immediately. Additionally, since it would be his condition that the Israelis would find difficult to fulfill, the Palestinians could not be blamed. If it had been the Palestinians that came up with a negotiation-killing condition, it might have impacted their ability to gather enough support for a U.N. statehood vote. It was the unfortunate Mitchell who would have to carry the new condition into the process, a negotiator bringing a condition that prevents negotiations, the paradox of duplicity. Editorialists would write how silly the president was, even incompetent, to inject a new condition between the conflicted parties, criticism from which Obama's media apologists would defend him. The ploy worked, the parties ceased talking and Obama could pretend, without much media scrutiny, that he was doing all he could.

Meanwhile, the Palestinians would, for the first time, begin the process of being approved by the United Nations as an entity ready for statehood, the sudden start to this effort beginning not long after Obama took office. That way, when the time for the U.N. vote would arrive in exactly two years just as the Palestinian "prophet" Fayyad's bold prediction indicated, there would be no technical reason to not grant statehood.

But Obama's plan would hit a snag in April 2011, with the Israeli leader invited to speak before Congress, offering him a platform that would be heard around the world. Should he offer some new, bold peace plan to the Palestinians, which was expected, U.N. members wavering on the statehood vote might give negotiations another chance. Concerned, Obama had to react quickly. The only sure fire way to prevent Netanyahu's speech from placing the Palestinians on the defensive, and possibly stopping the upcoming U.N. vote, would be for the president to give one of his own. However, it would be necessary for the president to announce his plan first, not allowing Netanyahu the positive media exposure to be garnered by a new Israeli proposal. If Netanyahu had been allowed to present his plan first, the media pressure to give it a chance would have been too great. If after such a speech Obama dismissed it, even as Netanyahu broke new ground, he would risk exposure that even his media allies could not protect him from. Therefore, the only way to prevent that from happening was to deliver his speech prior to Netanyahu's. The second essential part for Obama related to the contents of the speech. Obama had to make certain that his new policy was so far away from anything that had any chance whatsoever of being accepted, that it would finish negotiations for good, eliminating the main threat to a U.N. vote. That explains the awkward rush to get his plan out so quickly, even at the risk of looking petty, as though it was a one-upmanship game. But Obama was not playing a game.

Having delivered a speech laying out a draconian new policy against Israel that the Jewish state could not possibly accept, the ploy worked; and Netanyahu did not bother delivering his new plan which was now dead-on-arrival. But by taking so radical a position against Israel, Obama also accomplished another major goal. He lined up U.S. policy with the U.N. vote for Palestinian statehood along the lines of the 1967 borders.

Then another fly landed in the ointment—George Mitchell. As a statesman, Mitchell could not be pulled into Obama's plan. When, in early April, Mitchell found out what the new Middle East policy entailed, essentially abandoning America's alliance with Israel, he obviously balked. Obama, not wanting to lose any of his "team" before the big move coming in the following month, must have attempted to convince Mitchell to stay. Eventually, Mitchell, seeing that Obama intended to go forward with it anyway, abandoning Israel and killing negotiations for the second time in just two years, made his move. Obama almost certainly would have asked his resignation letter be released *after* the speech. But wanting no part in the release of the new policy, Mitchell insisted it be done *before*.

Now, two options have opened up for Obama. The first option is a straight U.N. vote, establishing the nation of Palestine within the severe 1967 borders wherein the U.S. Ambassador abstains, thus allowing the U.N. Security Council to pass the nationhood resolution. After such a vote the pressure on Israel will mount tremendously to comply with the wishes of the world community, setting it up as a pariah nation in the eyes of the world. That, however, runs a risk for the president as he heads into the 2012 presidential election, opening the possibility of losing his critical block of Jewish voters and their financial support. No doubt he has carefully studied the Jewish reaction to his speech of May 19 to determine if that is a viable option. If it is not politically feasible, then he can alter his approach and exercise a second option. That option is to allow his new draconian policy to hang over the head of Netanyahu, or any future Israeli leader, as a great hammer of pressure to force compliance with his new harsh standard that is now impossible to pull back from without Israel incurring even greater political damage. In this option he vetoes the

U.N. Palestinian statehood option. Then, if reelected, he allows it to go through in his second term. The first option is worse for Israel, the second not too far behind. The pincer movement is complete.

Would an American president that courts the Muslim Brotherhood, an enemy of Israel, undermines long time U.S. ally Hosni Mubarak, a peaceful nation on Israel's border, but is hesitant to undermine the long time U.S. enemy Syria, an enemy on Israel's border, be capable of such a plan? That is for you, the reader, to decide. President Obama is the first anti-Israeli president since the Jewish state's rebirth. As a result, the year 2011 has come to represent a time of the greatest threat to Israel, and her continued possession of the land since the war of 1948.

In 1993, as the Oslo Peace Accords were being negotiated from April through August, coincidentally "one of the most significant and damaging natural disasters ever to hit the United States" also took place, unfolding from April to August, month by month alongside the negotiations. With an array of such coincidences taking place since 1991, many occurring to the very day a "peace" effort started, an obvious question should be raised. Since April 2011 marked an important turn in U.S. policy against Israel, and a great new threat to the Promised Land, what, if any disaster was experienced within the United States?

CHAPTER NINE

History's Worst Tornado Rampage

As the spacecraft streaked across the heavens, people the world over looked to the stars that day. The "final frontier" was finally being explored, even if it was only a brief 88 minute step into it. Exploring it had become a contest, of sorts, one that both the U.S. and Soviet Union believed the benefits of winning would prove to the world whose system of governance worked best. It was, however, the bristling weapons of both countries that threatened the very viability of the planet the astronaut excitedly viewed from the small window of his craft that day. America's first man to orbit the Earth watched with fascination the sight of the world below. The view from his spaceship was breathtaking, experienced by only an elite few, including the Russian Yuri Gagarin and Alan Sheppard, the first American into space. John Glenn would be the first American to orbit the Earth in his NASA craft named Friendship 7.[1]

The view of Earth from so high above allowed the identification of continents, and during the short night of an orbiting astronaut, the bright lights of great cities provided the rarest of entertainment for its audience of one. In the light of day, the shape of islands, bays, and lakes could be seen, and above them swirling clouds interspersed throughout blue skies. Also, as though looking at a life size topography map in a high school geography class, the great rivers of the world were clear as anything displayed by a teacher, their complicated networks of tributaries visible as well. While passing over the United States, he could see the arteries leading to the mighty Mississippi including such great rivers as the Ohio, Missouri, Tennessee, Arkansas along with the Illinois and Red Rivers. Each of those major rivers had its own significant network of tributaries adding to the flow that eventually spilled into the Mississippi. As the Obama administration was making its historical change in policy toward Israel, endorsing the 1967 borders and lining up its plan with the United Nations statehood plan to be voted on in September 2011, another development began unfolding in the United States that would ultimately have a great impact on those same river systems.

Around the time Obama's new policy against Israel had apparently been decided upon, something began to happen inside the United States. Beginning on April 4 a severe weather system, an extremely large squall line tracking across almost the entire southern U. S. began to make its violent presence known. With the system came winds as high as 90 miles per hour. In just Tennessee and Georgia, nearly 250,000 homes lost power. However, along with the severe weather came 40 unwelcomed guests, tornados across the United States, mostly in the southern region, began striking. April 1 through 3 had been free of the twisting menaces. However, on April 4 it all began.[11]

As April progressed, large numbers of tornados continued to strike across the U.S., hitting the following states: West Virginia, New York, Arkansas, Kentucky, Tennessee, Ohio, Louisiana, Mississippi, Georgia, North Carolina, Maryland, California, Virginia, Indiana, Nevada, Iowa, Wisconsin, Missouri, Texas, Alabama, Oregon, Oklahoma, Kansas, Illinois, South Carolina, Pennsylvania, and Florida. Between April 14 and 16, 162 tornados struck a variety of southern states. In Sanford, North

Carolina, an intense tornado badly damaged businesses and destroyed 30 homes, with 2 people losing their lives. In the Askewville, North Carolina area, a twister that measured 1/2 -3/4 miles in diameter traveled an 18-mile path, creating widespread damage destroying many houses, mobile homes and businesses. Numerous homes were reported being ripped off of their foundation. The terrible stories would be replicated across the South. After the rampage was over, Alabama Governor Robert Bentley and North Carolina Governor Bev Perdue declared a state of emergency in their respective states. In Oklahoma and Mississippi, 26 and 14 counties, respectively, were placed in a state of emergency.[12][13]

Within those same three days, other severe weather activity took place. Late-season blizzard conditions were experienced in Kansas, Nebraska, and parts of North Dakota, with up to 16 inches of snow and high winds. Northeast New York State experienced very high winds, with gusts up to 70 miles per hour, causing damage throughout the area. And the tornados continued.[14]

After those 162 tornados in just three days, what happened next would be historical, making the initial rampage pale in comparison. Tornados had continued their random strikes across the southern region of the U.S. since April 16. But beginning on April 25, the worst would truly hit. From April 25 until April 28, the United States experienced 327 confirmed tornados. Due to some confusion in counting, it is possible there were even more. By the end of the four day rampage, all tornado records were broken, with the loss of life hitting 344 people. The financial damages just from the tornados added up to $10 billion. It would represent the largest tornado outbreak in United States history, impacting the South, Midwest, and Northeast and leaving catastrophic destruction in its wake. It also brought with it other thunderstorm-related destruction, including hail and flash flooding. As the fronts that would spawn the tornados entered an area, they would often produce a phenomenon called "thunder gusts." These gusts of wind on the leading edge of the thunderstorms often had winds of up to 80 miles per hour and over the four days, they would add their frightening presence to the tornados' already historical impact.[15]

After April finally ended, both the record books and history books needed to be opened. April 2011 concluded with 875 confirmed tornados. To put that in proper perspective, the previous record for any April in U.S. history was 267. In fact, the previous record for tornados in any month in U.S. history was 542, which happened in May 1993.[16] The April 25-28 outbreak is believed to be the largest four-day outbreak in world history. According to the National Oceanic and Atmospheric Administration (NOAA) concerning weather in April:

> April was a month of historic climate extremes across much of the United States, including: record breaking precipitation that resulted in historic flooding; recurrent violent weather systems that broke records for tornado and severe weather outbreaks; and wildfire activity that scorched more than twice the area of any April this century....the world's two largest tornado outbreaks in history: April 25-28 and April 14-16. Incredibly heavy rains also resulted, with six states along the Ohio River and Mississippi River recording their all-time wettest April in history.[17](emphasis added)

Indeed, the tornado outbreak in April 2011, as indicated by the National Oceanic and Atmospheric Administration, included "...the world's two largest tornado outbreaks in history."

The historically severe weather added so much rainfall that it began to impact the nation's river systems as well. In the northern states of Montana, North and South Dakota, and Wyoming, governors began calling up hundreds of National Guard soldiers to create sand bags in an effort to hold back rising waters. The effort to thwart Mother Nature included the building of temporary levees as well. The problem facing the region was two-fold. The winter had brought record amounts of snow-fall in the Rocky Mountain range and its inevitable melting caused rivers and tributaries to overflow. But adding to the already dire situation were significant amounts of rainfall. In some areas, the record flooding would cut off a town, necessitating emergency workers to ferry food and water to its trapped citizens.[2]

In Yellowstone County, Montana, *The Billings Gazette* reported that the flooding was only comparable to the deluges of '75' & '78', both historical in their own right for that part of the country. Ultimately, flooding in some parts of North Dakota would break the record set in 1881.[4] But the flooding in the northern parts of the U.S. would pale in comparison to what was happening further south.

Memphis, Tennessee would experience record flooding, producing fear that the levees might not hold back the deluge, possibly impacting famed musical landmarks Graceland and Beale Street. The Mississippi River would ultimately crest at 48 feet, coming within less than a foot of the all-time record set from the devastating 1927 flood.[5] In the exclusive neighborhood of Harbor Town located in downtown Memphis, over 5,200 residents would have to be evacuated as the water rose to levels never before seen. In Dyersburg, located in the northwestern part of the state, over 600 homes and businesses would become inundated as a tributary of the Mississippi flowed backwards into the city.[6]

In the state of Mississippi, weather officials had projected crest levels at both Vicksburg and Natchez above the record 1927 levels, and Ole' Man River would not disappoint. In Natchez, the mighty river set a new record at 58.48-feet, with the water level surpassing that of all previous recorded flooding. Neighboring Vidalia, just across the river, was terribly impacted by the river's rise, facing economic disaster and mass evacuations. In spite of dealing with its own historical flooding, Natchez would extend a hand of help to its sister town. The flooding in Natchez and other places impacted some of the most fertile areas in the country, with damages to agriculture reaching at least $2 billion. In Vicksburg, on May 19, a new record was set with the crest reaching 64-feet as the river's water raced south at over 1.5 million cubic feet per second.[7,8] Army Corps of Engineers spokesman Kavanaugh Breazeale observed that one particular levee, being overtopped, had not experienced that happening since the 1927 flood. More than a dozen casinos dotting the riverfront area were shuttered as the flood waters continued to rise.[9]

For the sake of saving both Baton Rouge and New Orleans from the massive tide of rolling crests heading south, the Morganza Spillway was opened for the first time since 1973. But there would be a price to pay for exercising this option. Downstream from the spillway, resting in the path of the rushing waters lived 25,000 people. Now they were forced to leave their homes and businesses. The impact to Louisiana would be massive, with spillway waters inundating three million acres. The decision to open the spillway pitted the cities of Baton Rouge and New Orleans against small rural towns. Had the spillway system not been utilized, the massive tide of water might have breached the New Orleans levee system, replicating Katrina. Having little choice, the larger cities won: the governor ordered the opening. Further north in the previous month, city slickers had also won against country folk, with the Army Corps of Engineers blowing up a levee in Missouri, flooding farms there to save the city of Cairo, Illinois. It was indeed a dangerous flood.[10]

Before it was all over, the Mississippi River floods in April and May 2011 would compare only to the other two great deluges in the last century, the great floods of 1927 and 1993. Significant flooding would occur in Illinois, Missouri, Kentucky, Tennessee, Arkansas, Mississippi, and Louisiana. It was a deluge of historic proportions.

* * * * * * *

It is necessary to briefly look back at the resignation letter tendered by master U.S. diplomat George Mitchell. As was pointed out in the previous chapter, Mitchell, who had been the lead man for American efforts between the Israelis and Palestinians since the Clinton administration, resigned weeks before Obama announced his new policy against Israel. Interestingly, although there is little doubt the president must have wanted the resignation letter released to the media *after* the new draconian policy against the Jews was announced, it was, in fact, released *before.* This had to displease the president, indicating disunity within his foreign policy ranks just as the radical shift in policy against Israel was about to be announced. Therefore, Mitchell must have insisted upon this. As a master diplomat and understanding the art of subtlety, Mitchell had to know the message he was sending by releasing his resignation letter *before* the president announced his new policy, that he not only had nothing to do with its creation, but opposed it. His action, in fact, indicates a strong disagreement since no diplomat wants to offend his president, especially a diplomat as prominent as Mitchell. But he did it anyway. The only thing that could have caused Mitchell, a man of honor, to do such a thing to his president, would have to involve a policy disagreement so egregious that he would want to disassociate himself from it completely, just as the Democratic leader in the U.S. Senate, Harry Reed, would do. Perhaps remembering that early in the administration, the president had injected a new condition on the Israelis, killing negotiations, Mitchell finally experienced his epiphany.

Since we know from the *New York Times* that Mitchell's resignation letter was dated April 6, but not released until five weeks later, just before the president's speech, we can logically deduct that the new policy came out sometime just before April 6. Further, since Mitchell, through his actions sent a clear message of strong disagreement with the new policy, it is reasonable to conclude that his resignation letter came quickly, probably within a day or two, once he realized what the new approach to Israel was to be. Based on the above logic, it would appear U.S. policy turned strongly against Israel and the Promised Land she held sometime very early in April, probably around the 3rd, 4th or 5th. Based on weather reports, we know that the worst tornado rampage in world history began on April 4, 2011.

* * * * * * *

As April's tornados began, destined to make history, interestingly, the previous record of the most tornados in the U.S. was 542 that began its historic rampage on April 30, 2003, the first day the international group the Quartet (*four horns*) met. Its purpose was to pursue the removal of large tracts of the Promised Land from Israel in the name of "peace." The ancient prophet Zechariah had warned of a time when a group of four would come together to remove the land from Israel, indicating their efforts would be met by the Biblical *craftsmen* that promised to *fray* the nations involved in this action. That tornado rampage, representing what weather experts called the "worst weather in U.S. history," was immediately followed by the worst heat wave in over 250 years striking Europe, another main Quartet player. Then, in July 2007, within hours of Quartet envoy Tony Blair beginning the next Quartet effort, the world banking system began an unraveling that eventually became the global financial meltdown, bringing the world financial system to the brink of systemic collapse.

* * * * * * *

GEORGE W. BUSH'S DECLARATION

As egregious as President Obama's May 19, 2011 speech was, it only followed on the heels of George W. Bush's ground breaking move declaring U. S. support for the establishment of a Palestinian State that was to be announced the week of September 10, 2001. The issue at stake is a simple one. As serious as the various efforts to remove Israeli control over the restored land have been, effectively attempting to reverse a promise from God to the restored Israelites from a Scriptural point of view, the act of creating a Palestinian state on the land represents an action of a greater magnitude. It is comparable, in a sense, to people questioning your title to land granted you, and then deciding to actually build their house on it. As the next chapter shows, the fate of leaders that have succeeded against the Promised Land has been a difficult one.

CHAPTER TEN

The Fate of Leaders

As the prime minister stepped onto the platform, his gaze stretched across the sea of people before him, a thronging crowd numbering in the hundreds of thousands. The gathering represented an impressive display of support for the increasingly unpopular Oslo Peace accords. Yitzhak Rabin, only the fifth prime minister in the short history of the newly restored Israel, had shaken the hand of Yasser Arafat, leader of the terrorist organization, the Palestine Liberation Organization, less than two years earlier. And with that shake the Oslo Peace Accords between Israel and the Palestinians became a reality. The accords did what force-of-arms could not, removing Israeli control over large tracts of the Promised Land restored to Israel through war. In return, Arafat and the Palestinians promised to stop terrorist attacks targeting Jews. But the peace promised by the accords would prove fleeting, in fact, as fleeting as the life of the prime minister that agreed to relinquish the control.

Having finished addressing the crowds with what would be his last speech, Rabin turned for his car. As he began making his way down the steps of Tel Aviv city hall, he headed for the open door to his car, which would soon whisk him away from the rally. But before he got to the vehicle, three gun shots rang out, two striking the prime minister and fatally wounding him. The newly restored Israel had just lost its first leader to assassination.

In a sense, the fate of Rabin echoed that of another Israeli leader that ruled some three thousand years earlier. It was King Saul, whom the prophet Samuel had warned to obey the Lord's admonition to go to war against the Amalek tribe and to utterly destroy them. This tribe had been one that opposed the Israelites' trek to the land of Canaan after Egypt set them free. Saul's disobedience in the matter cost him his kingship to David. Essentially, like the ancient Egyptians who themselves had suffered greatly for the same reason, the Amalek had attempted to prevent the Jews from reaching the land of Canaan, in fulfillment of God's promise to them. The Divine wrath accorded them would be delayed, but not forgotten. Although Saul would remain king for a number of years, tormented by David's existence, he would eventually lose his kingdom and life just as Samuel had warned. But the notice from the prophet that Saul's days were numbered was given after that act of disobedience. It is important to note that the act of disobedience was associated with having not properly dealt with those whose ancestors had attempted to negatively impact the Israelites possession of the Promised Land. Rabin, however, was engaged in removing that same land from Israeli control. Perhaps Rabin's assassination was again just another coincidence, but there would be more such coincidences impacting other leaders.

The Oslo Peace Accords were considered a breakthrough for the "land for peace" movement that believed Israel's enemies could be pacified with land. As covered in the previous chapter, Rabin agreed with this and willingly acted as the leader of Israel to relinquish Israeli control over lands promised them by the Lord. Those lands were restored in stages. The first of the lands was restored in 1948 during the War for Independence, and later in 1967 during the Six-Day War. It was the land restored in 1967 that Rabin had agreed to give up control over.

As in the case of King Saul and Prime Minister Rabin, the following Scriptures appear to apply.

> *But God is the judge: he putteth down one, and setteth up another.* (Psalm 75:7) (emphasis added)

> *And he changeth the times and the seasons: he removeth kings, and setteth up kings:...* (Daniel 2:21) (emphasis added)

But a bad fate for those leaders that molested the Promised Land would not be limited to Rabin. As indicated in the previous chapter, from April 1993 through August 1993, as Rabin was negotiating away Israeli control over areas of Judea and Samaria, "one of the most damaging natural disasters ever to hit the United States" unfolded month by month, with negotiations that led to the accords. It had been the policy of the U.S. to pressure Israel into relinquishing control over the areas promised them in the ancient Hebrew Scriptures, in the name of peace.

* * * * * * *

Yitzhak Rabin had served two terms as Israeli prime minister, first assuming the post in 1974, and then once again in 1992. It was during that first term that he chose former Major General in the Israeli Defense Forces Ariel Sharon as his advisor for security. Sharon had been involved in fighting for the Jews in Palestine ever since 1942, when, as a fourteen year-old, he had joined the Haganah, an underground military organization formed to protect Jews in the dangerous region of their ancestors. In February 2001, Sharon became prime minister of Israel. Viewed as a hawk and not a believer in the "land for peace" process, he received significant support from the Israeli electorate that agreed with that view. However, under increasing pressure from his friend in the White House,

George W. Bush, Sharon surprised ally and foe alike by agreeing to relinquish the land of Gaza to the Arabs living there. And on August 23, 2005, the removal was declared complete by the Israeli Foreign Ministry.[1]

Of course, on that very same day, August 23, 2005, the National Weather Service would spot Hurricane Katrina, which was destined to remove hundreds of thousands, including this author, from their homes. However, that was not all that happened.

On December 18, 2005, a little under four months from the completion of the removal of Gaza from Israel, Ariel Sharon suffered a stroke. He would return home several days later in a slightly impaired condition. But that stroke was only a precursor to another that would occur less than three weeks later. On January 6, 2006, Sharon suffered a massive stroke, leaving him in a vegetative state. Now, over five years from that day, in his quasi-comatose state, he can open his eyes when spoken to or pinched, according to Raanan Gissin, former Sharon spokesman.[2] However, that is all he can do.

* * * * * * *

U.S. President George W. Bush had, indeed, developed a close relationship with Sharon. So close, that Prince Abdullah, ruler of oil rich Saudi Arabia, had commented about the relationship between the two, saying that "what Sharon wanted, he got" from Bush.[3] The impact of Hurricane Katrina would extend well beyond damage to the Gulf Coast, reaching all the way to the White House. In late 2008, near the end of the Bush Presidency, two top presidential aides would explain it best. Referring to Katrina, Matthew Dowd, Bush's pollster, would explain its political impact on Bush this way:

> The president broke his bond with the public. Once it was broken, he no longer had the capacity to talk to the American

public. State of the Union address? It didn't matter. Legislative initiatives? It didn't matter. P.R.? It didn't matter. Travel? It didn't matter.[4]

No matter what Bush did, it had no positive impact on the public after Katrina, and the perception that he did not respond quickly enough. The other White House aide, former Communications Director Dan Bartlett, observed, "Politically it was the final nail in the coffin."[5]

And indeed it was. Ultimately, Bush's response to Katrina would start a decline in his popularity that became irreversible, sending his poll numbers into the low twenties. For Bush, who had engineered the successful removal of a portion of the Promised Land from Israel, the disaster of Katrina would result in his own political disaster as well. Although it is a rarity that a natural disaster would effectively cripple a presidency, there is another case of such an event contributing to the demise of another American leader.

★ ★ ★ ★ ★ ★ ★

Just over eight years before his son would win the presidency, George H.W. Bush would experience his own natural-disaster-turned-political-disaster, just prior to the 1992 presidential election. What, at that time, would be the most costly hurricane in U.S. history, Andrew, struck just as President Bush was convening the opening session to another round of the Madrid Peace Conference. Unlike the previous conferences, however, Bush had a willing Israeli Prime Minister in Yitzhak Rabin. As a result great progress was made that eventually led to the September 1993 Oslo Peace Accords, where large tracts of the Promised Land were removed from Israeli control. President Bush would go on to lose the November election to Bill Clinton, in a campaign where Clinton made Bush's slow response to the victims of Andrew an issue.

In the days following the storm, countless Florida residents were left languishing in the sun with little food or water. Adding to the president's political misery were reports coming from the Pentagon that large amounts of emergency supplies were ready for immediate shipping to the affected area, delayed by presidential hesitation.[6] As the national media, caught up in the presidential election frenzy picked up on the story, one storm victim after another began lashing out at the president on national TV. When the votes were counted, Clinton had been elected president.

Perhaps Bush should have known that engaging to remove the Promised Land was dangerous. The year before, on the very same day his administration had successfully engineered the first breakthrough, the Madrid Peace Conference, the Perfect Storm slammed the New England coast. Also, and on a personal level, as the president was at the opening session in Madrid, a 30' wave from the storm swamped his Kennebunkport, Maine home, severely damaging it and washing the Bush furniture out to sea. Apparently, he missed the omen.

CHAPTER ELEVEN

The Increasing Severity of the Warnings

I f the "coincidence" of catastrophes relative to *advances* against the Promised Land represents a Divine warning to mankind, then something new must be added to the equation. As will be demonstrated in this chapter, the severity of disasters has increased since its beginning in 1991. Perhaps that represents a final type of warning from the Divine, a last effort to gain the attention of man as he moves inexorably toward that which is forbidden by his Creator. If this is what it represents, then President Obama's actions since taking office represent a great danger for America. Since the rebirth of Israel in 1948, the current efforts by Obama to establish a Palestinian state have exceeded the worst fears of the most paranoid supporters of the Jewish state. In fact, his May 19, 2011 speech, wherein he essentially took the Palestinian position against Israel, represents more than just a strong move against the land. It reaches the threshold of a threat against the existence of the Jewish state, making it vulnerable to attack once again. Prior to the president's watershed speech, his Middle East actions had already created a dire threat against Israel's very existence. By undermining moderate Egypt, Israel's friendly neighbor, and then taking care not to undermine Israel's enemy, Assad of radical Syria, Obama's actions have essentially revived the old threat against Israel, the one that had been removed by the courage of Anwar Sadat in signing the Camp David Peace Accords. Undoubtedly, his actions in this regard since taking office represent the most egregious threat ever against Israel. Once Obama's goal has been achieved Israel will be caught in a "pincer movement," surrounded on all sides by her enemies and abandoned by her oldest friends.

So are the disaster "coincidences" becoming more severe? Here is a financial analysis in seven year increments.

FROM 1991 UNTIL 1997

- October 30, 1991 The Perfect Storm

It was called a "once in a hundred year storm" for the way in which it formed and how it struck.

$1 billion

- August 24, 1992 Hurricane Andrew

It was the most costly hurricane in U.S. history at that time and extremely destructive. The financial cost would run about

$30 billion[1]

- The 1993 Great Flood

It was one of two great floods to hit the U.S. in 100 years.

$15 billion[2]

- January 17, 1994 Northridge Earthquake

It was the highest instrumentally recorded earthquake in an urban area in U.S. history.

$25 billion[3]

TOTAL COST $71 BILLION

FROM 1998 UNTIL 2004

- June 5, 2001 The Great Texas Flood

  The most destructive tropical storm in U.S. history.

  $5 billion

- September 11, 2001 Terrorist Attack

  Estimated the cost in dollars at

  $843 billion[5]

- April 30, 2003 562 Tornadoes

  "The Worst weather in U.S. History"

  $5 billion[6]

- June to August 2003 European Heat Wave

  The worst heat wave in 250 years.

  $10-20 billion[7]

TOTAL COST: $863 BILLION

FROM 2005 TO 2011

- August 23, 2005 Hurricane Katrina

  An incomparably destructive storm.

  $165 billion[8]

- Week of July 23, 2007 "Global Financial Crisis"

The week that it all started, culminating in a near systemic collapse in 2008. The International Monetary Fund estimated cost:

$10.2 Trillion[9]

- April 20, 2010 "Gulf Oil Rig Disaster"

Estimates are between

$32-40 billion[10]

- April 2011 "875 Tornados & Historical Flooding"

Estimated damages:

$26 bilion[11,12,13,14,15]

TOTAL COST: $10.42 TRILLION

Even when accounting for the loss of value in the U.S. dollar over that period of time the fundamental picture stays the same. Each seven year interval has seen a significant increase in the cost associated with the disasters within it. As such, if this dramatic increase represents a culmination of Divine warnings, then the actual result of establishing a Palestinian state should bring a response on an order of magnitude greater than the warnings, since seldom are warnings greater than what they warn about. When considering the magnitude of the disasters reviewed, such a final event would have to be cataclysmic, possibly resulting in a fundamental change in the world power-matrix.

At the conclusion of *The Israel Omen,* a matrix called the "Political-Catastrophe Matrix" was constructed. It presented what actions against the old prophecies would result in a matching destructive event. So far, the "Matrix" appears to have held up to the test of time. The latest example being the litany of anti-Promised Land moves since the beginning of the Obama Administration culminating in his May 19, 2011 speech wherein he presented his plan for the land promised in the ancient texts to the Jews.

★ ★ ★ ★ ★ ★ ★

Perhaps all of these historically severe calamities have been nothing more than a series of coincidences, often happening to the day an effort *advanced* against Israeli control of the lands promised in the Scriptures. That is, of course, possible. But those series of coincidences began on October 30, 1991, when the first President Bush launched the Madrid "peace" process, just as the infamous "Perfect Storm" was striking a bewildered New England coast. *The Israel Omen* took the reader from that 1991 opening of the "peace" process until 2008, covering ten historically severe events that coincided with the efforts to remove the land. But at the end of that book was a question mark. Would the phenomena continue? Three years down the road we know the answer to that question with three more historically severe "coincidences" able to be added to the litany of the original ten. With the Gulf Oil Rig Disaster, the Iceland volcano, and the tornados of April 2011 now history, there is a question begging to be answered: have all of these events been a Divine warning, and if so to what are they leading? That question is especially pertinent as President Obama appears ready to go to any length to establish a Palestinian state along the lines desired by the Palestinians. In answer to that question, certain Biblical prophetic passages eerily appear to apply to the litany of strange "coincidences" that have been taking place since 1991, and carrying with them a strong warning for America and the world.

CHAPTER TWELVE

A Prophetic Foreshadowing

The windows rattled furiously as sheets of rain ripped across the old English mansion located not far from the Channel. Across that body of water separating the British Isles from the European continent, waves 20-and-30 feet high were challenging the best efforts of sailors. Outside, soldiers of every rank scurried about attending to their business as if Mother Nature's gale force winds were a figment of their imagination, their tasks too important to be interrupted. The mansion, named Southwick House, had recently been appropriated by the Allies as their headquarters to direct the Expeditionary Force soon to begin the greatest invasion in world history. Inside, its highly decorated occupants listened to hear every word their leader spoke. With the raging summer storm swirling about the house, General Eisenhower stood at the center of another storm, one that he and those awaiting his decision knew would impact the fate of Western Civilization. The Allied army was coiled like a spring and ready to jump across the English Channel, ready to face combat with Hitler's finest in a test of wills that would determine the fate of Europe, and the outcome of the Second World War. A defeat on the heavily guarded beaches of France due to choppy seas would be a historic catastrophe, the blame going to the general who made the decision. The question Eisenhower faced was a simple one, should the Allied invasion force be launched against the Nazi war machine in France, or should it be postponed for a second time due to weather? A postponement this time would, in reality, mean at least a fortnight delay awaiting proper tidal and moon conditions, and there was no guarantee that weather conditions would be any better then. After asking each of the generals their opinion, it was now Eisenhower's turn to speak, uttering words that would alter the course of history. The room was silent, its occupants suddenly unaware of the raging storm engulfing the house.

In their younger years many of those in the room had participated in the First World War, a war promised to end all wars only 26 years earlier. That war had, in a way, been a foreshadowing of the current life and death struggle whose epicenter now could be traced to that room, in that house near the southern coast of England. Perhaps some in the room mused in the privacy of their thoughts how it could have come to this, after having beaten the Germans in the First World War. But whatever thoughts they entertained as they waited in silence, Eisenhower would soon speak words that would change everything; "Ok, let's go." With those three words the invasion of France began, ultimately leading to Hitler's defeat and the end of the Second World War.

* * * * * *

Occasionally, in the course of history, a significant event takes place that foreshadows a similar, but greater event yet to happen sometime into the future. In hindsight, the First World War was a precursor, or foreshadowing, of the more severe Second World War. Both had Germany as the main antagonist, millions died, and maps changed significantly in their aftermath. In the First World War, the Germans had the Kaiser; in the Second they had the Führer, which was much worse. In the First, tragically, 16,500,000 were killed; in the Second 62,000,000. In the First, all of Europe was set ablaze—in the Second, Europe, North Africa, and the Far East.[1,2]

In the Biblical realm, there is such a thing as a foreshadowing as well, with the character Antiochus Epiphanes immediately coming to mind. Many Bible scholars view him to be a type of foreshadowing of the terrifying world leader expected at the end of the age. Epiphanes, who came to power in Syria in 175 B.C., completed numerous prophecies reserved for the coming world leader, but certainly not all of them.[3] However, his foreshadowing is useful in glimpsing into the terrible nature of the feared world leader Christians are assured will arise.

For those whose faith is placed in the ancient words of the Holy Bible, there is a sense of knowing mankind's destiny, even understanding the train of events that will come to pass during a time of unparalleled upheaval. Reassured by past prophetic utterances that have unfolded according to the Divine script, logic adds its weight to faith assuring the believer that the remaining prophecies will come to pass as well. It is from this perspective we consider *The Israel Omen's* warnings as a possible foreshadowing of a much larger event yet to come.

Within the diplomatic efforts covered in *The Israel Omen* and *The Israel Omen II,* a common denominator exists, actually three of them. The first is that they all were based on the belief that if a settlement between the Israelis and Palestinians can be reached, then "peace" will finally be achieved. Since 1991, when the diplomatic effort against the land began, the litany of talk about "peace" is well documented. Since 2003, when the Quartet (*four horns*) took over the effort, they have spoken many grand proclamations about how "peace" will result if only Israel will give up the land. However, it is important to make the distinction between the perception of "peace," and the reality of such. To any observer of the region whose opinions are shaped by results, the notion that true "peace" will result from the removal of the land is a difficult one to embrace, especially when the case of Gaza is examined. As is well recorded after the Israelis withdrew from Gaza, thereby leaving it to the Palestinians, rocket attacks originating from there against Israeli civilian targets increased dramatically. Essentially, the result from implementing the idea of "land for peace" was more conflict, not peace.

But sometimes politicians ignore results, especially when those results interfere with policy, and the Quartet's effort is clearly one of them. According to those promoting the "land for peace" concept, "peace" will be the result if the land is given up, regardless of previous results. An educated guess tells us that most of the media embraces this idea, especially within the United States. Based on the length of time that the conflict has raged, and the importance of the Middle East to the world, should a "peace" treaty be achieved between the Israelis and Palestinians, grand proclamations will be heard announcing that Middle East peace has finally come. Excalibur will have been pulled from the stone.

The second common denominator is an obvious one, the historically destructive nature of the events and how they coincided with those diplomatic efforts to remove the land. None of those disasters covered in *The Israel Omen* and *The Israel Omen II* were minor, but rather, historical, setting them apart and adding to the eerie nature of the "coincidences." The third common denominator is how swiftly the diplomatic efforts were followed by destruction. Here is a litany of events worth reviewing for the swiftness of the destruction that followed. The Perfect Storm struck the first day the conflicted parties gathered in Madrid, Spain. Hurricane Andrew struck the first day they met in Washington, D.C. The "worst natural disaster in U.S. history" began the week negotiations started and ended with them. The Northridge Earthquake struck the day President Clinton pressured Prime Minister Rabin to return the Golan Heights. Tropical Storm Allison quite suddenly formed just off the Texas coast within a few hours of the announcement against the Promised Land. It was during the week of September 10, 2001 that the Bush Administration was planning to announce support for the creation of a Palestinian state in the middle of the Promised Land. It was the first day of the first Quartet (*four horns*) meeting that the historical rampage of tornados representing "the worst weather in U.S. history" began. Then the worst heat wave in 250 years began immediately after that weather ended. On the exact day of the announcement the Israeli withdrawal from Gaza was completed, Hurricane Katrina was first identified. Then, the same week that the Quartet (*four horns*) launched its effort for the second gathering of nations against the Promised Land, the banking system suddenly began an unraveling that ultimately led to the financial meltdown. The Gulf Oil Rig explosion happened within 0-3 days of a new advance against Jerusalem. The Iceland volcano blew its top the day the ASA handed down its decision against Jerusalem. And finally, the incredible weather of April 2011 appears to have begun within 0-3 days of Obama settling on his new draconian policy against Israel.

Notice how the timing of the disasters was immediate relative to the various moves against the Promised Land. Or, put another way, as diplomats were talking about "peace," there was sudden destruction. In fact, in almost all of the disasters, the destruction that immediately followed the efforts toward "peace" was historic. That degree of uniqueness separates these disaster events from others that commonly take place over the course of time, as though nature is expressing its disapproval. Since 1991 the litany of events has been similar to a broken record repeating the same phrase over and over again: peace, then sudden destruction... peace, then sudden destruction... peace, then sudden destruction... and so forth as if nature is being directed in an attempt to gain the attention of mankind. This brings us to the notion that *The Israel Omen*'s events may be alluding to another, much larger event yet to happen. Essentially, what is approaching may be a foreshadowing of an even larger event to occur sometime in the future.

There are numerous Scriptures that tell of a time when God will pour out tremendous wrath upon the world, and it is referred to as the day of the Lord. That event appears to take place deep into the foretold *times* and, therefore, it is not just around the corner. But *The Israel Omen* events have an uncanny resemblance to Scriptures relating to it, raising the possibility that they are warning that, perhaps, some kind of a lesser cataclysm is approaching that many years from now, with the benefit of hindsight, may be viewed as having been a foreshadowing of the day of the Lord. This is speculation, but look at the Scriptures relating to the day of the Lord versus what has been happening. This from 1 Thessalonians...

> *...For you yourselves know perfectly that the day of the Lord so cometh as a thief in the night. <u>For when they say, Peace and safety; then sudden destruction cometh upon them</u>, as travail upon a woman with child; and they shall not escape.* (1 Thessalonians 5:2-3) (emphisis added)

We are told that *the day* comes suddenly, *as a thief in the night*. So the Scripture is telling us the event that will happen is completely unexpected by people, like that of a thief appearing inside a home in the middle of the night. Thieves are totally unexpected. Yet, immediately after that statement we are told when this will happen. It will happen *when they say, Peace and safety*. The two statements appear to be in contradiction, one saying the destruction will take place *as a thief in the night*, implying it will be a big surprise to people, and the other telling us when it will happen. But the solution to that really is quite simple. Those with Biblical understanding will not be surprised by the event, those without Biblical understanding will be. Since we are told what to look for in order to be ready for what should be a global cataclysm, we should expect the signs to extend to the entire world so that Believers everywhere will be able to recognize the sign of *when they say, Peace and safety*. Otherwise, if it was an event only significant to a region or country, Believers in the rest of the world would be at a devastating disadvantage. Since the *peace* event should be one that both impacts the world as well as one that Believers would be attuned to, that leaves only the Middle East. With Israel reappearing in the land of their ancestors, Christians across the world have marveled at the event with many proclaiming that a prophetic clock began on the day of its rebirth.

When some kind of agreement finally that takes place between the Israelis and Palestinians, almost every nation on the planet would see it as a great achievement toward *Peace and safety*. Indeed, the Quartet (*four horns*) leading the effort has brought together nations and regional organizations from across the globe to become involved in the process. The best example of this was seen during the Annapolis Quartet Peace Conference in November 2007. At that conference 45 nations and international organizations attended. A settlement of the conflict between the Israelis and Palestinians would remove a potential flashpoint that could disrupt oil supplies coming from that region. *Peace* there would bring relief to nations everywhere as the threat to the flow of oil is diminished. Because of the dependency of almost all nations on oil, there has always been the potential of World War Three starting in the Middle East, with its impact threatening the entire world. This, too, would be diminished and welcomed by the entire world. There is a third concern shared by the world relating to the Middle East, the threat of terrorism. That threat has impacted almost all nations, and many believe it would be reduced if the dispute between the Israelis and Palestinians is resolved. The theory in support of that goes something like this. One of the big issues used to recruit by al-Qaeda and other terrorist organizations is the cause of the Palestinian Arabs for nationhood. Once resolved, the recruits will dry up and terrorism will begin to abate over time. Since the killing of Osama bin Laden, along with many other top al-Qaeda leaders, the sense that the age of terrorism may be coming to a conclusion will increase appreciably should there be a "resolution" to the Israeli-Palestinian conflict. So it appears that *when they say, Peace and safety* must to refer to the Middle East, the location of where the Scriptures proclaim Israel is the apple of Gods eye.

Continuing from 1 Thessalonians...

But ye, brethren, are not in darkness, that that day should over-take you as a thief. Ye are all the children of light, and the children of the day: we are not of the night, nor of darkness. Therefore let us not sleep, as do others; but let us watch and be sober. (1 Thessalonians 5:4-6)

As is always the case, God watches over His own, those that love and follow Him. As such we are told not to *sleep, as do others* so that we can identify the signs leading up to this event and can be prepared. We are also exhorted to *watch and be sober.* Obviously, since we are told to *watch* there is something to *watch* for, a sign that Believers who are *sober* will see so that they can understand that, in fact, the time of *when they say, Peace and safety; then sudden destruction cometh upon them* is drawing near. Now a question should be considered. What sign would be the clearest for the Believer to see, but missed by the World? Perhaps the clearest message would be a litany of repeating events, minor when compared to what is approaching, but clear in their consistent message. The message might be something like this; peace...then sudden destruction; peace... then sudden destruction; peace... then sudden destruction over and over again to gain the attention of as many as possible. However, these warning events would have to be on a much smaller scale then the approaching cataclysm they warn about, allowing the Believer to prepare adequately for the coming event. Considering the historic nature of the events that have constituted these warnings, what could possibly be worse? Perhaps another Scripture in 2 Peter that relates to the day of the Lord gives us some clarity.

> *¹⁰But the day of the Lord will come as <u>a thief in the night</u>; in the which the heavens shall pass away with a great noise, and the elements shall melt with fervent heat, the earth also and the works that are therein shall be burned up.* (2 Peter 3:10) (emphasis added)

Clearly this passage is referring to the same event as the one in 1 Thessalonians, referencing *the day of the Lord* and further acknowledging that it will come suddenly like *a thief in the night*. But more details are provided here as to the nature of the coming event. This sudden event will apparently begin *with a great noise*, after which a tremendous fire of a kind powerful enough to melt the elements *with fervent heat* will follow. Then one verse later the description continues.

> *... Looking for and hasting unto the coming of the day of God, wherein the heavens being on fire shall be dissolved, and the elements shall melt with fervent heat?* (2 Peter 3:12)

There is provided here a detailed description of the event in question. The descriptions of this event appear to clearly describe what happens after the detonation of a nuclear weapon. There is a *great noise* associated with the explosion, then the *elements shall melt with fervent heat, the earth also* resulting in *the works that are therein* are *burned up*. Sadly, when considering the historical nature of the "coincidences" associated with the efforts to remove the Promised Land from Israel, it is difficult to find another event whose magnitude would appropriately conclude the culmination of warnings since 1991.

It is important to note that the speculation here is not that the *day of the Lord* is about to happen, but that the litany of events possessing a consistent message is a warning that a foreshadowing type event might be approaching. Then the question arises as to what the possibilities of such a dire event happening in the relatively near future are, one with the potential represented by the aforementioned Scriptures. In regard to that question, Part Two, "The Unspoken Threat to America" attempts to provide an answer.

PART TWO

The Unspoken Threat to America

CHAPTER THIRTEEN

The New Threat

At first they came by the dozens, brave souls risking it all for a land they could only imagine in their dreams. Then they poured in by the thousands. As rumors spread that the Soviet Empire was breathing its last gasp of life, the enslaved began heading toward the wall, the Berlin Wall, the ultimate symbol of tyranny, holding captive the vanquished of the Second World War. Like Lilliputians sensing the giant's moment of vulnerability, they headed for the wall in droves. Older Berliners, who had long suffered its existence, could reflect on a time when a dashing young American president had immortalized words within its hideous sight, even declaring in their native language himself a Berliner. John F. Kennedy's death after that memorable day would bring forth tears from his fellow Berliners, only exceeded by those of his fellow Americans.

There is only one "day that will live in infamy" and only one "giant leap for mankind." But in the case of the Berlin Wall, a second American President would immortalize words within its dark shadow. Ronald Reagan's admonition to the young Soviet dictator to "...tear down this wall" would nudge the domino that eventually took down the entire empire behind it. The "evil empire" Reagan so reviled was finally heading to the "ash heap of history" that he had assured the world was its destiny.

As the thousands leaving East Berlin for the freedom of the West turned into tens of thousands, the tens of thousands soon became 100,000 per hour. In Moscow, the Soviet leadership, sensing that the dyke of oppression had broken, accepted the inevitable. Germany was free and united as in days past, before the time of Hitler. As their empire collapsed around them in the ensuing months, it soon became their turn to experience revolution. However, the beginning of a revolution often does not reflect its ultimate outcome. As slavery within the empire's borders turned into freedom, that freedom soon morphed into chaos and with it, the joy of the West turned into fear.

As a nation teeming with nuclear weapons, the Soviet Union could destroy the United States several times over, and, of course, in so doing bring about its own destruction with an American retaliatory nuclear strike that was sure to follow. This paradox of warfare, peculiar to the twentieth century, was the result of a concept designed specifically for the advent of the nuclear age. Appropriately christened with the acronym M.A.D., standing for "mutually assured destruction," the doctrine virtually guaranteed that as a Soviet nuclear strike was unfolding against the United States, American missiles of mass destruction would be approaching their Soviet targets. With neither nation capable of surviving such an exchange, and caring more about its own survival than the destruction of its enemy, doomsday never happened. Finally, with the breakup of the Soviet Union, it appeared that mankind had made it past the horrors of nuclear conflict. To many in the West, the atomic swords could now be beaten into plowshares.

But occasionally events take a cruel turn and usually when it is least expected. Little did western observers in those heady days of 1991 understand that the very event they were cheering would ultimately bring about an even greater threat than the one their old Soviet nemesis presented. In addition to the demise of the Soviet Empire, something else had changed in the nuclear threat matrix, and few observers at the time even noticed.

* * * * * * *

With the collapse of Communism, the transformation to Capitalism was a difficult one for the people of the former Soviet Union. By 1996, with economic conditions in a severe decline, poverty, unemployment, inflation, and suicide rates all rose dramatically. Because of the economic depression, the birth rate in Russia, the main former Soviet republic, dropped significantly, resulting in an actual decline in the population. After having a military measured in the several millions of troops, the new Russian military declined significantly in both numbers and strength. Because of a lack of adequate funding, it is estimated that over 100,000 in the military lacked proper housing. Both soldiers and the highest ranking officers seldom received a regular paycheck, with many being forced to beg.[1]

Against this dreary backdrop of decay and disarray efforts were being made to secure thousands of nuclear weapons at facilities across the massive expanse of the former Soviet Union. Recognizing the potential of loose nukes resulting from the Russian chaos, the U.S. Senate passed the Nunn-Lugar Soviet Threat Reduction Act designed to provide funding and technical assistance to Russia for securing nuclear weapons. One of the key goals was to secure the removal of the weapons from the ethnic Muslim former republics, bringing them to secure sites within Russia. The Secretary of Defense at that time, Dick Cheney, would indicate before a congressional committee that success of the program would be defined as securing at least 90% of the weapons at large. That, however, would leave unaccounted for approximately 220 nuclear weapons, all substantially more powerful than those used against Japan in 1945.[2]

With nuclear scientists finding it difficult to feed their families, and the military men in charge of guarding the nuclear facilities experiencing poverty, the two formed a dangerous combination. This was especially true since a fully operational nuclear weapon, or even a small amount of highly enriched nuclear material, would bring a king's ransom on the increasingly active nuclear black market. Even if a dozen soldiers and scientists colluded in the effort, the money for each in such an exchange would not only lift them out of poverty, but make them wealthy. The results of this temptation began showing very quickly.

In his excellent investigative book, *The Al Qaeda Connection*, Paul Williams points out that, in 1992, shortly after the demise of the Soviet Union, an Egyptian newspaper reported that Iran bought three Soviet nuclear warheads from the Muslim dominated former republic of Kazakhstan for $150 million. Disturbingly, this report was later confirmed by Russian intelligence. But that was not all. Later, in 1993, two more Russian nuclear warheads were stolen but then later recovered. In the criminal case that followed, the chief Russian prosecutor said what many security minded individuals were beginning to realize, that "potatoes were guarded better" than nuclear materials within the former Soviet Union.[3]

★ ★ ★ ★ ★ ★ ★

It had been over six years since the breakup of the Soviet Union when in September 1997, the renowned TV news magazine program *60 Minutes* had just finished airing an interview with Russian General Aleksandr Lebed, former Secretary of the Russian Security Council. It was an interview that left many viewers shocked and concerned. Among the many responsibilities of the council's members was oversight of the vast Russian nuclear arsenal. That particular responsibility was made especially difficult because of the chaos that followed the 1991 revolution. It did not take a professional observer to understand that chaos and nuclear weapons do not mix. But, nonetheless, they had mixed. In the interview, and earlier that year before members of a US Congressional delegation, Lebed revealed a new and very dangerous threat to the Western nations. He claimed that the former Soviet Union had manufactured about 132 very small nuclear weapons, referred to as atomic demolition munitions (ADMs) that were designed to be very small to allow Soviet Special Forces to bring them behind enemy lines. As a result of the mission for which they were developed, the ADMs had to be made as light weight as possible. To accomplish this, the standard safety devices to prevent unauthorized detonation were not added to them. Because of their small size and portability, many in the West began referring to them as "suitcase" nukes. He went on to point out that "some" of the "suitcase" nukes had been forward deployed in various former Soviet republics, and frighteningly added that they might not have been returned when the Soviet Union began to crumble. Some of those former Soviet republics included Turkmen, Uzbek, Tajik, Kirghiz, and Kazakh, all with large ethnic Muslim majorities.[4] Then, attempting to be even more specific, he stated that while he could confirm that at least 132 of these "suitcase" nuclear weapons had been produced, he knew of only 48 that could now be accounted for. The following exchange between CBS correspondent Steve Kroft and General Lebed is revealing. Referring to the small, "suitcase" designed missing nukes:

KROFT: But, it's already in a suitcase"?

LEBED: Yes.

KROFT: I could walk down the streets of Moscow or Washington or New York, and people would think I am carrying a suitcase.

LEBED: Yes, indeed.

KROFT: How easy would it be to detonate?

LEBED: It would take twenty or thirty minutes to prepare.

KROFT: But you don't need secret codes from the Kremlin or anything like that?"

LEBED: No

Then, a little later in the interview:

KROFT: So you are saying these weapons are no longer under the control of the Russian military?

LEBED: I am saying that more than one hundred weapons are not under the control of the armed forces of Russia. I don't know their location. I don't know whether they have been destroyed or whether they are stored or whether they've been sold or stolen. I don't know.[5]

Coming from someone whose job it was to know the whereabouts of these small nuclear bombs, the revelation was all the more disturbing. Russian official reaction to Lebed's statements was quick and derisive. A spokesman for Russian President Yeltsin declared Lebed's revelations were the "product of a diseased imagination." Prime Minister Viktor Chernomyrdin declared the allegations "absolutely false." Former officials of the Soviet military as well as atomic energy indicated that no such bombs were ever made, and went as far as to say that they did not even have the technology to miniaturize nuclear weapons to such a degree. But as the denials continued, they began to take on a contradictory tone, ultimately serving to add fuel to the concerns raised by *60 Minutes*.[6]

There was something else that appeared hollow in the official Russian denials. During the Cold War the US and Russia essentially possessed similar nuclear technology and capabilities, and yet the US had manufactured hundreds of suitcase size nukes in the 1970s. Therefore, the denials that the Soviet Union did not possess the technology to accomplish miniaturization rang false. Additionally, claims by a "presidential advisor" that ADMs had been built for KGB Special Forces to operate behind enemy lines, lined up with U.S. understanding of the Soviet wartime strategy of creating diversionary actions.[7]

★ ★ ★ ★ ★ ★

Secret agents of the Dutch intelligence service, the AIVD, hurried through the evening streets of Amsterdam, their destination being a quiet suburban neighborhood just outside the city. Finally arriving at the address, accompanied by a multitude of uniformed police, they quickly descended upon the house. The occupants within the residence hear the frantic nature of the knocks on the door, with one series quickly succeeded by another. The elderly couple inside move slowly, their pace belying an anticipation of what awaits them on the other side. As the door is opened, they immediately see a multitude of officialdom before them, their identifications waving. It is not the aged couple that has drawn the attention of so many Dutch agents, but their daughter.

Leaving the elderly couple to be watched by the uniformed police officers, the agents proceed to search for the young female they know should be in the house. To their relief they find her upstairs, but with a bemused look on her face. She appears strangely unmoved by all of the commotion, with an attitude bordering on expectation of their arrival. She is asked to produce a letter that they say she recently received from abroad. Immediately, and without the slightest protest, she produces an unopened letter from her dresser drawer. The young woman, Kausar Kahn, is immediately whisked away to police headquarters, along with the letter that will be a source of great angst to Western governments and their allies across the globe. It presents a frightening revelation written by her uncle, the infamous "nuclear salesman" A.Q. Khan.[8]

The letter is immediately passed on to high officials of the Dutch government. Shortly afterward a facsimile arrives in Washington, D.C., where it is studied, confirming what Washington had suspected for some time. It contains a series of revelations from Pakistan's most famous scientist and national hero. It was Dr. Abdul Qadeer Kahn that had mastered the science of creating for his homeland the most feared weapon of all time, the nuclear bomb. Capable of destroying an entire city in a micro second, it provided his fellow Pakistanis' with a counter threat against their mortal enemy, India. No longer could Pakistan be threatened by its more populous neighbor. It, too, could now return a devastating blow with the push of a button. Thus, the scientist that developed it was etched in the hearts of his fellow countrymen as a national hero. Although a hero to the people of Pakistan, Kahn was now on a collision course with the government of his country and now a virtual enemy of the feared Inter-Services Intelligence (ISI), Pakistan's brutal internal security agency.[9]

The letter detailed the policy of a generation of generals and political leaders that used Pakistan's much coveted nuclear secrets as a bartering chip to enhance the nation's diplomatic efforts. Details in the letter listed the government's more notorious clients which included North Korea, Libya, and Iran. It read like the business plan of Nuclear Proliferation, Inc. North Korea paid $3 million for nuclear drawings and machinery, while Libya received centrifuge components. Iran also received drawings, components, and the names of nuclear suppliers. But as disturbing as these accusations were, the decision of how to deal with Pakistan's flagrant disregard for the spread of nuclear weapons had actually been resolved almost four years earlier on September 11, 2001.

In the days of decision that followed the attacks on the World Trade Centers and the Pentagon, the Bush Administration concluded that one of the top priorities in the new "war on terror" would be to have the full cooperation of Pakistan. Situated next to Afghanistan where the war would soon be prosecuted, it could become a safe haven for al-Qaeda and its notorious leader, Osama Bin Laden, unless it became a U.S. "ally" in the war effort. In late 2001, the Bush Administration secured the "cooperation" of Pakistan. As a result, both countries adopted the same story line concerning nuclear proliferation originating from Pakistan. It was the "notorious" A. Q. Khan that, for the love of money, had spread the deadly technology abroad. But according to Kahn, in revealing his side of the story to *The Sunday Times* investigative reporter Simon Henderson, he was only following the policy dictates of his government. The much sought after letter held by his niece in Amsterdam was his effort to set the record straight, a record that neither the governments of Pakistan nor the United States could now afford to acknowledge. But regardless if it was Kahn acting on his own, or on behalf of the Pakistani government in risking the lives of countless millions in pursuit of temporary diplomatic gains, one thing was certain. The nuclear genie was now out of the bottle, and like its Soviet counterpart, it would never again be returned. However, unlike the nations that had crossed the nuclear threshold before them, the first Muslim nation to do so had quickly become a willing merchant of doom.[10]

* * * * * * *

After the arrest of Khalid Shaikh Mohammad, mastermind of the September 11 attacks, what he had to say during his "enhanced" interrogation sent shivers down the spines of those listening. As al-Qaeda's military operations chief, his captured laptop computer held a treasure of information that was as disturbing as it was informative. Within it was documentation of meetings between Dr. Khan and Osama bin Laden for the expressed goal of creating a "nuclear hell storm" within the United States. Under questioning, Dr. Kahn revealed that this was the top priority of al-Qaeda and that those involved in the project answered only to bin Laden, al-Qaeda co-leader Ayman al-Zawahiri, and a mysterious scientist called "Dr. X." According to additional testimony from Mohammad and other al-Qaeda witnesses, bin Laden described his intentions in even more chilling detail, indicating al-Qaeda's goal of detonating nuclear bombs in seven strategic locations throughout the country, effectively ending the United States as an organized nation state. [11] [12]

Assessing the nuclear threat to America from al-Qaeda, General Eugene Habiger, formerly in charge of U.S. strategic weapons, put it this way. It is "not a matter of if, but when" such a terrible event happens.[13] Former Vice President Dick Cheney would add to Habiger's concerns, stating that a nuclear attack from al-Qaeda within the United States appeared to be imminent.[14] Adding their voices to the chorus of concerns, both former U.S. Attorney General John Ashcroft and Homeland Security Director Tom Ridge would express their fears that al-Qaeda might succeed in the near future with his dastardly plan to bring nuclear destruction to America.[15]

* * * * * * *

As President Mahmoud Ahmadinejad, the Iranian leader, stands before the United Nations General Assembly, his mission is to alert the world leaders to the unfolding spiritual conflict in the world, according to his mind. He fulfills it. It is perhaps the most spiritual speech ever given by the leader of a nation since the founding of that world body. Then, two months later, reminiscing about his speech, a video captures the Iranian leader telling a cleric that he felt the hand of God entrancing world leaders as he spoke to them. A month after the video, while commenting on the loss of 108 fellow Iranians aboard an airliner that crashed in Teheran, he points out that "what is important is that they (the dead) have shown the way to martyrdom which we must follow."[16]

He is a follower of the Hidden Imam, the Messiah-like figure of Shia Islam believed to have gone into "occlusion," or seclusion, in the ninth century at the age of five. Also known as the Mahdi, he is destined to lead the world into an era of universal peace after the tumultuous "Last Days." It is believed that his return will be preceded by unprecedented worldwide death and destruction, and Ahmadinejad believes the time is close at hand. Except, unlike the Christian version of the "Last Days," the "Twelvers," as they are referred to, believe they can hasten the savior's arrival by creating the cataclysmic conditions foretold. He and his country are also feverishly seeking nuclear weapons.[17]

Iran and its leader would have to credit the nuclear smuggling network established by A.Q. Khan with the success of their nuclear program. In the late 1980s, Khan used articles in technical journals to demonstrate his knowledge of how to build a nuclear bomb. This caught the attention of the Iranians, who ultimately became his first customer. Coincidentally, this took place as relations between Pakistan and Iran were warming, giving support to Khan's later accusations that it was his own government that had him front for them in proliferating nuclear technology as a diplomatic tool. Regardless of who was ultimately behind the effort, Iran received nuclear technology assistance in 1987. Then, as the 1990s progressed, Khan's nuclear network became a place where, for the right price, virtually anything necessary for the development of a nuclear weapon was available.[18]

By 2003, the Khan network had become transnational, spanning over seven countries including Pakistan, Switzerland, Turkey, South Africa, Malaysia, the United Kingdom, and the United Arab Emirates. It was also able to boast North Korea as a client state, a regime led by another demented leader. The Kahn network had shown it was capable of dealing with the devil, and demonstrating no remorse about it. With both North Korea and Iran possessing the ability to enrich uranium to levels capable of producing a nuclear weapon, there was no guarantee they would keep it confined to their borders.[19]

Nuclear proliferation by the likes of North Korea and Iran is at the very least very destabilizing. But it is the widespread suspicion that the network helped al-Qaeda obtain nuclear secrets before the collapse of the Taliban in Afghanistan that raises the nuclear specter to a new level of concern. Motivated by pan-Islamism and hostility to the West, Khan had traveled to 18 countries between 1997 and 2003, in an apparent effort to find clients for his services. Of all of the countries visited, the most worrisome was Afghanistan. During the time that Khan visited, both al-Qaeda and the Taliban were still in charge, still working hard to form the perfect Muslim state, one that would have been undistinguishable from its predecessors of 1,000 years ago.[20] Yet, in spite of the great move away from advanced civilization taking place within the borders of that rugged state, the Khan network of advanced nuclear technology did business there.

Documents obtained in October 2001 revealed that Dr. Sultan Bashiruddin Mahmood, a colleague and friend of A.Q. Khan, and chairman of the Pakistan Atomic Energy Commission, had met with al-Qaeda's Osama bin Laden, and second in command al-Zawahiri in Afghanistan. After being taken into custody by the efficient Pakistani Intelligence Service, and several weeks into "intense" interrogation, Mahmood began to talk. He admitted that he had met with the two terrorists, as well as other al-Qaeda officials to discuss an atomic blast in an American city. He added that bin Laden was quite serious in creating what he called an "American Hiroshima," nuclear destruction within America and that al-Qaeda already possessed fissile material obtained from the Islamic Movement of Uzbekistan and that they were in the process of perfecting nuclear weapons. Mahmood would lead investigators to another scientist from the notorious nuclear network that reportedly worked with al-Qaeda, Dr. Chaudry Abdul Majid, the chief engineer of the Pakistan Atomic

Energy Commission. He, too, would give his interrogators an earfull of fear, indicating that al-Qaeda's interest in meeting with him related to the construction and maintenance of nuclear weapons.[21][22][23][24]

* * * * * * *

In November 1994, Dzokhar Dudayev, leader of the rebels operating within the former Soviet Republic of Chechnya, indicated to the world that he possessed nuclear weapons and requested United Nations assistance in the form of troops to protect them. This odd request was viewed as an effort on the part of Dudayev to gain much coveted media exposure for the Chechen cause. Apparently, realizing no one was taking his request seriously, he provided a demonstration the world could not miss. After planting a bomb made of cesium-137 in Izmaillovsky Park in Moscow, the rebels directed a television crew to its location. The TV crew discovered it, essentially verifying that the rebel leader was deadly serious. But that incident was only a precursor to the main attraction. The rebels then informed the United States that they were in possession of suitcase tactical nuclear bombs, and then proceeded to issue a stark ultimatum to the world's lone superpower. Recognize Chechnya's independence from Russia, or they would sell the weapons to a rogue nation or to al-Qaeda. Confirming the viability of the threat was the National Intelligence Council, an umbrella organization for the U.S. analytical community. It indicated that, indeed, nuclear materials, as well as small "suitcase" type nuclear weapons were missing from the Russian stockpile.[26]

In January 1996, a Russian presidential advisor informed the Monterey Institute's Center for Nonproliferation Studies that in the 1970s, an unspecified number of ADMs had been manufactured for the KGB. Additionally, another presidential advisor, Aleksey Yablokov informed a Congressional subcommittee in October 1997 that he was "absolutely sure" that ADMs had been built for KGB special forces. Then he added that these weapons were not included in the Russian Ministry of Defense nuclear weapons inventory, nor covered by its accounting and control systems. Then, in the summer of 1995, in another nuclear revelation appearing to confirm Lebed, the Russian press had published several articles indicating that Chechen separatists had either obtained some of the suitcase nukes, or were attempting to. Had some of these terrifying weapons made their way into the hands of al-Qaeda? Perhaps that question was answered in 2001.

A report by two British undercover agents raised the threat level for nuclear proliferation to a new level. As recruits from a London mosque in 2001, the two special agents of British intelligence infiltrated an al-Qaeda training camp in Afghanistan. The confidential report went on to say that after completing all training, they were both sent to the town of Herat in western Afghanistan for a special operation. While there, they were given the opportunity to visit an al-Qaeda laboratory. They later reported that within the laboratory they observed scientists and technicians working on a sophisticated nuclear weapon that they developed from radioactive isotopes.[27]

EVIL INTENT

What the brilliant Albert Einstein had theorized, scientists Ernest Walton and John Cockroft had accomplished, splitting the atom for the first time in a controlled experiment and thus unleashing that primordial force of nature. That accomplishment, which would ultimately assist in ending the Second World War with the development of the atom bomb, would later add to its reputation by creating power necessary for generating electricity for entire cities, bringing comfort to the lives of countless people across the globe. But great power can be difficult to control and often becomes a two-edged sword, as was with the splitting of the atom. The sword unsheathed by that singular scientific discovery has enabled small groups to enjoy the power usually reserved for entire nations, but without the same responsibility.

With the radicalization of Islam and the formation of al-Qaeda, the other side of the sword has grimly begun making itself known. Not satisfied with the death of thousands on September 11, 2001, al-Qaeda has remained coiled, waiting for the next big strike that is certain to come. Having gained the coveted attention of the world with the destruction of the World Trade Centers and Pentagon, it is now planning another attack that is even larger and more deadly. With the power to destroy entire cities in a mere microsecond now miniaturized, it is reasonable to fear that the next big event will be nuclear. Within the realm of warfare technology presents a great dilemma. It has been used to benefit masses of people across the globe, bringing great hope. But by its very nature it allows small groups to muster its massive power to control those same masses of people.

The paradox is stark and has been most notable in the twenty-first century. Since the beginning of civilization, the nation state has been the most powerful entity possible, bringing together large numbers of homogeneous people under an organized government. But that has now changed. In the case of a nation state so foolish as to use a nuclear weapon, especially against another atomic state, it cannot find protection by hiding itself and runs the risk of retaliation guaranteed to bring great harm upon itself. However, when it comes to nuclear terrorism from a stateless organization such as a terrorist group like al-Qaeda, the counterweight of nuclear destruction simply does not exist. By an order of magnitude, a nation is not as inherently dangerous as the stateless jihadist organization with crazed beliefs and a willingness to die. Therefore, to truly understand the risk America faces, there are some very unpleasant realities that must be considered. The potential availability of a nuclear weapon either purchased or made after securing the radioactive material necessary to construct them has been shown to be a legitimate possibility. However, possessing such power is not enough, there must also be the intent to use it. Although there are other radical Islamic terrorist organizations in the world intent on doing harm to the "Great Satan," it is al-Qaeda that has succeeded. In understanding the intentions and beliefs of the organization, we begin to understand the extent to which America and the West is at risk. It is truly a clash of civilizations.

* * * * * * *

Statements from Osama Bin Laden and other terrorists have made their intent clear as it relates to both the acquisition and use of a nuclear weapon. In spite of bin Laden's death at the hands of U.S. Navy Seals, it can be assumed that his statements over time have represented the general beliefs of the organization as a whole. In an interview with reporter John Miller, shown on ABC News, bin Laden answers a question as it relates to his organization's efforts to acquire nuclear weapons. This in December, 1998:

> Acquiring weapons for the defense of Muslims is a religious duty. If I have indeed acquired these weapons, then I thank God for enabling me to do so. And if I seek to acquire these weapons, I am carrying out a duty. It would be a sin for Muslims not to try to possess the weapons that would prevent the infidels from inflicting harm on Muslims.[28]

Then he is asked if he is worried that America has called him Public Enemy Number One. His words are telling

> Hostility toward America is a religious duty, and we hope to be rewarded for it by God. To call us Enemy No. 1 or 2 does not hurt us. Osama bin Laden is confident that Muslims will be able to _end the legend of the so-called superpower that is America._[29] (emphasis added)

Asked again about his reported efforts to acquire nuclear weapons, he renews a previous fatwah, stating, "If I seek to acquire such weapons, this is a religious duty. How we use them is up to us."[30]

In February 1998 bin Laden declared in an edict:

Despite the great devastation inflicted on the Iraqi people by the crusader-Zionist alliance, and despite the huge number of those killed, which has exceeded **1 million...**"[31] (emphasis added)

It is important to note that bin Laden claims U.S. troops fighting in Iraq have killed one million people there. Being an obviously false number, he uses it just the same. It is clearly not for Western consumption, however, but for Muslims. Such statements appear to be an effort to create a moral justification for some future action against American civilians where a large number are killed. He went on attaching God's will to his efforts to kill Americans:

We with God's help call on every Muslim who believes in God and wishes to be rewarded to comply with God's order to kill the Americans and plunder their money..."[32]

Efforts on the part of al-Qaeda to develop nuclear capability began in the early 1990s. Prior to the September 11 attacks, testimony in a federal trial relating to the 1998 African embassy bombing revealed an attempt made in late 1993 into early 1994. Jamal Ahmad Al-Fadl, an al-Qaeda operative testified that he was involved in efforts to acquire uranium in Sudan. The uranium in question was purportedly already enriched and the three foot long container purportedly housing it bore a "South Africa" label. Al-Fadl indicated that he had seen the container and knew that $1.5 million had been paid for it. After that, his involvement ended.[33] Later, it was discovered that the deal was a scam. The report that it was a scam is open for speculation. But one thing is certain: al-Qaeda was actively pursuing nuclear weapons.

Then in 1998 German authorities arrested Mamdouh Mahmud Salim, a bin Laden associate, charging him with trying to obtain highly enriched uranium. Later and possibly related to the Salim incident, Arabic media began reporting that bin Laden was spending millions of dollars in an attempt to obtain nuclear weapons. The report went on to say that he was hiring nuclear scientists from Turkmenistan and Iraq. Turkmenistan had been part of the former Soviet Union. Its scientists no longer needed and finding employment difficult, were indeed vulnerable to being recruited. It was also reported that he was offering cash to both Russians as well as Chechens for "suitcase" nukes as well as nuclear material. Israeli intelligence, perhaps the finest in the world, confirmed the reports concerning bin Laden's attempts to purchase a "suitcase" nuclear weapon.[34]

In December of 2001, only three months after the tragic day of September 11, the Russian state nuclear agency confirmed that within the last two years there had been "a major incident involving the attempted theft of nuclear materials." Also in that month Pakistan reported that Osama bin Laden had met with Sultan Bashiruddin Mahmood and Abdul Majid, both former high ranking scientists in Pakistan's nuclear program. The revelation included the fact that Mahmood had been dismissed from his post because he had been advocating sharing nuclear weapons with other Islamic states. But reassuringly, for those that would believe it, both insisted they had only discussed humanitarian issues with the man responsible for the deaths of thousands on September 11. Pakistani interrogators, finding the story unbelievable, began using more convincing interrogation methods, finally resulting in the two admitting they had discussed nuclear, chemical, and biological weapons with bin Laden.[35]

In line with his efforts to acquire nuclear weapons, in May of 1998, bin Laden issued a statement titled, "The Nuclear Bomb of Islam."[36] In it he explains how Muslims have a duty to acquire nuclear weapons and terrorize the enemies of God. In a 2007 video, he promised "to use massive weapons" to destroy Capitalism and help create an Islamic caliphate. His chief lieutenant, Ayman al-Zawahiri, was quoted in 2001 as saying in an interview, "If you have $30 million, go to the black market in central Asia, contact any disgruntled Soviet scientist, and dozens of smart brief-case bombs are available."[37]

CONCLUSION

The primary factor that had made the Cold War a manageable test of wills was the nature of the enemy. As dastardly as the Soviets could be, one thing was certain, they intended to survive. In a strange sense, it was that very basic rational belief system which acted as a sort of unseen hand moderating its acts of provocation. It was only during the administration of Jimmy Carter that the Soviet invasion of Afghanistan took place. Understanding the man in the White House, they apparently believed there was little chance he would act forcefully against them. But when it came to a strong president, like Nixon or Reagan, they acted with much more care not to press too hard. With the fall of the Soviet Union, and the rise of Pakistan as a nuclear power, that uneasy equation began to change. Combined with the gathering of Islamists dedicated to the destruction of the West, especially the United States, under the banner of al-Qaeda, the world has become a much more dangerous place.

CHAPTER FOURTEEN

Breaching the Border

I t had been only one month since the al-Qaeda terrorist organization had flown jets loaded down with fuel into the Twin Towers of the World Trade Center and the Pentagon. A fourth hijacked plane had been prevented from reaching its target by the courage of its passengers, overwhelming the terrorists in a fight for survival on board the plane. That jet would crash in a field in Pennsylvania with all on board losing their lives. Its intended target, either Capitol Hill or the White House, had been spared. The nation, still reeling from the shocking events of that day, began to realize that the nation was in a very real war with an enemy that could hide by blending into its host country.

Hoping to prevent such a day from ever happening again, the president and his administration began, on September 12 to formulate a strategy for the United States response. But on the morning of October 11, 2001, President George W. Bush would receive information that shocked him. It was a revelation that would alter the perceived threat to the nation that he led, raising it to the highest level possible. CIA Director George Tenet had arrived to give the president his daily intelligence briefing, which since 9/11 had taken on greater urgency and significance.

What the CIA Director would tell the president that particular morning would change everything.[4]

In the underworld of spies and informants, a catchy name to identify them appears to be a requirement. Because in many cases the life of the individual hangs in the balance, they would prefer that their real names never be used. Although at times the code names given appear to have come from Hollywood, their message often is not. In the case of "Dragon Fire," the message was not only serious, but frightening. From somewhere within the shadowy netherworld of spies, a CIA agent relayed the message that al-Qaeda possessed a 10-kiloton nuclear bomb, reportedly stolen from the Russian arsenal. As bad as that was, the next part was even worse. The bomb was purportedly already within New York City.[5]

Should a nuclear detonation take place within Times Square, it would instantly annihilate everything within a half a mile of its ground zero. The next zone of destruction would be within a mile from the point of detonation where buildings would crumble, fires would rage, and radiation would be severe. The initial death toll would quickly reach 250,000. Within a month, due to the volume of serious injuries and radiation poising, that number would likely reach 500,000. The economic toll would hit $1 trillion. However, the economic aftershocks could conceivably collapse the U.S. financial structure, the ultimate financial costs from such an event too high to calculate. It would be a truly devastating act that could alter the course of American history.[6]

The president immediately ordered Vice President Dick Cheney to establish an alternative government at a secure and undisclosed location. Along with the vice president went hundreds of federal employees from a dozen key governmental agencies. This action was according to a standing government plan enacted in the event of a threat to the nation's capital, insuring that if a nuclear weapon was detonated, it would not decapitate the leadership of the nation.[7]

In the hours that followed the Tenet briefing, a special nuclear emergency team was sent to New York City to hunt for the nuke. The White House decided not to tell the mayor of the city, the colorful Rudy Giuliani, in order to avoid any chance of the news leaking and panic ensuing. Condoleeza Rice, the president's national security advisor, termed the predicament the "problem from hell." And, indeed it was.[8]

Months earlier the CIA's Counterterrorism Center had overheard chatter in al-Qaeda channels about an "American Hiroshima." That term was being used to indicate the nuclear destruction of an American city, or horrifyingly worse, several cities being destroyed at the same time. Those frightening words were spoken against the backdrop of the CIA's knowledge that Osama bin Laden had been attempting to acquire nuclear weapons since the early 1990s.[9] Now, the question of a nuclear attack had become much more than an academic exercise being played out in some war room. Had he succeeded? That simple question would plague the leadership of the world's only superpower for years to come.

Of course, we know a detonation never took place. But was there a nuclear bomb present in New York City just as Dragon Fire had warned? That question may never be answered. But another question has to be answered by those concerned for the future of America. Are our borders secure enough to make it improbable for al-Qaeda to bring a nuclear weapon within America? Concerning that question, there is this.

On the first anniversary of 9/11, *ABC News* decided to test the penetrability of U.S. Customs on the porous Mexican Border. Their plan was a simple one designed to give border agents the same chance to discover the news team's unsavory package as they would have to find the real thing if it came their way. The results would be telling and an indictment of border security since the attacks a year earlier.

To understand the *ABC News* operation, it is first necessary to understand the nature of uranium. There are two basic types of uranium:

highly enriched uranium (HEU) and depleted uranium (DU). Essentially, HEU is the type that is required to build a nuclear weapon. Depleted uranium is not at all useful in constructing a nuclear bomb. Both, however, emit a similar radioactive signature after HEU is covered with something as simple as an 1/8 of an inch of lead. Typically HEU will emit approximately 100 times the alpha radiation that depleted uranium does and the gamma-ray dose is about ten times. But again, when covered with a relatively thin lead shield the radiation signatures are roughly the same. With a fifteen pound cylinder of depleted uranium loaned by the Natural Resources Defense Council, *ABC News* attempted to smuggle it into the U.S. They were successful with it passing through the U.S. Customs checkpoint. To make matters worse, they did it again on the next anniversary, September 11, 2003. The lesson from the report was obvious: the U.S. was not prepared to stop a nuclear weapon from entering the country.[10]

If there is one thing TV news organizations enjoy doing it is to embarrass government agencies. U.S. Customs would become the target of yet another TV news team, this time out of Atlanta and nearly nine years after the attacks of 9/11. *WSBTV Channel 2 Action News* anchor Justin Farmer traveled to Arizona to visit the U.S border with Mexico in May of 2010. What he found was truly disturbing. In a pair of videos, the station exposed the magnitude of the threat faced at the U.S. southern border. Infiltration by individuals hailing from nations identified as breeding grounds for radical Islamic terrorists was rampant. The individuals in question are identified as "other than Mexicans," or OTMs. What the reporter and his news team discovered was that a substantial number of these OTMs have been apprehended attempting to cross the border. Dave Stoddard, a border agent for over 20 years, was asked how many of the OTMs are apprehended as they attempt to cross the border. After some thought, he indicated, "The American public has been kept in the dark about the issue...In my experience for every one apprehended, at least ten escape apprehension."[11]

Farmer pointed out the existence of a Congressional report titled "Line in the Sand: Confirming the Threat at the Southwest Border." This report confirmed that one of law enforcement officials' most wanted terrorist, Adnan El Shurkajumah of Saudi Arabia, entered the United States through Mexico and is now missing. Law enforcement officials also confirm in the report that members of the terrorist organization Hezbollah have entered through the southern border. Chillingly, the report cites the route of entry most taken by Middle Easterners to arrive in the U.S. is through Central America, indicating that first, they learn Spanish so they can blend in with the real Mexican illegal aliens.[12]

Mexico had detained 23 individuals originating from Somalia with ties to al-Qaeda that were eventually released. They, apparently, were heading for the U.S. border. The Obama Administration's response to the disclosures of OTMs entering the U.S. has been to cease releasing the information. Former U.S. Rep. J.D. Hayworth took a different view of the problem, stating, "We have left the back door to the United States open....We have to understand these are people who definitely mean to do us harm who have crossed that border." But the power to take action rested not with Hayworth, but with the president and his secretary of Homeland Security.[13]

Channel 2 News anchor Framer found documents in federal court in San Antonio indicating just how busy the terrorist activity on the southern border has been. The documents show an indictment of one Ahmed Muhammad Dhakane. The indictment accuses Dhakane of establishing a route from Brazil to Mexico used to bring OTMs close to the U.S. border. It specifically states that Somalis from the terrorist group Al Shabob entered the United States. According to Rep. Michael McCaul of Texas, "To this day we do not know where those 300 Somalis are...we do not know where they are in the United States." In observing the threat against the United States emanating from the southern border, retired immigration official Michael Cuttler says the threat is actually being covered up for political reasons. "Incredibly the government is attempting to keep the citizens like a bunch of mushrooms. Keep us in the dark and feed us a bunch of manure."[14]

The threat to America from the southern border has reached the attention of one of America's closest allies, and a constant victim of terrorist attacks itself. From Israel, Danny Danon, Deputy Speaker of the Israeli Knesset, revealed that there are training camps for Hezbollah terrorists supported by Iran and located along the border of Columbia and Venezuela. With the complete lack of security in South America against Islamic infiltration, these nations have become ripe as staging grounds for terrorists to enter into the United States.[15]

Former National Intelligence Director Mike McConnell told an interviewer, in 2008, that at least 30 Iraqis with terrorists ties were discovered attempting to enter the U.S. through Mexico. He went on to tell the reporter with the *El Paso Times* that, "There are numerous situations where people are alive today because we caught them." In April 2010, Homeland Security issued an intelligence alert that a Somali named Mohamed Ali, a suspected member of Al-Shabaad, a Somali-based al-Qaeda ally, was attempting to cross the border.

Signs that those OTMs crossing the border might not be doing so to enjoy the American dream littered the border landscape. Iranian currency was found in one place, in another, Islamic prayer rugs were discovered. Also found was a patch that reads "martyr" and "way to immortality." Yet another symbol found was a patch that shows a jet flying into a skyscraper.[16]

In the Congressional report, "A Line in the Sand: Confronting the Threat at the Southwest Border," the conclusion as to how numerous illegal entries into the U.S. have become is shocking. The following excerpts from the report drive home the vulnerability of terrorists entering the United States by simply walking across the border, bringing with them whatever they can carry.

During 2005, Border Patrol apprehended approximately 1.2 million illegal aliens; of those 165,000 were from countries other than Mexico. Of the non-Mexican aliens, approximately 650 were from special interest countries. Special interest countries are those designated by the intelligence community as countries that could export individuals that could bring harm to our country in the way of terrorism.

...Federal law enforcement estimates that 10 percent to 30 percent of illegal aliens are actually apprehended... Therefore, in 2005, as many as 10 to 4 million illegal aliens crossed into the United States...[17]

Based on the government's own estimates, only between 10 percent and 30 percent of illegal aliens crossing the border are apprehended, and within that number in 2005 were 650 such individuals from countries of special interest. Therefore, at least 2100 individuals from countries of special interest crossed the border into the United States in that year alone. That would be the minimum number, with the actual number probably much higher. Since September 2001, the number is obviously much larger, potentially presenting the United States with a possible "fifth column" within the country ready to fight when called upon.

But as serious a problem that security is on the southern border, it is the northern border with Canada that is beginning to worry some in Washington even more. U.S. Senate Homeland Security Committee Chairman Joe Lieberman revealed a study that showed the risk of terrorists crossing into the United States from Canada as being even greater than that from Mexico. This startling conclusion, he indicated "should sound an alarm, an urgent call for action." Lieberman unveiled a new report by the Government Accounting Office (GAO) wherein the U.S. Border patrol indicated that only 32 of the nearly 4000 miles of that border were at an acceptable level of security. The report also pointed out that an immediate arrest of individuals illegally crossing could be made along only 1% of the border. With the presence of Islamist extremists in Canada, US Department of Homeland Security views the likelihood of a terrorist crossing to be higher than from the Mexican border.[18]

With the borders having been left open since 9/11, and al-Qaeda seeking nuclear weapons with the intent of using them within the United States, the threat appears very real. The depth of the threat, however, is best understood by disturbing reports that have surfaced, some, but not all, being reported by major news services.

CHAPTER FIFTEEN

Disturbing Reports

As the Soviet ships approached the imprisoned island of Cuba, carrying their deadly cargo intended to tip the nuclear balance of the Cold War, U.S. naval vessels surrounding the island waited for orders directly from their Commander-in-Chief, John F. Kennedy. What the president did not want was for World War III to begin because some overly aggressive naval commander acted improvidently. For thirteen days in October 1962, the world waited, and wondered, if nuclear war between the two superpowers would suddenly begin, and bring with it an end to the world as it had been known.[1] In schools across the country air raid drills were practiced with students rushed into the school hallways, immediately assuming a position face down against any sturdy wall.

Civil defense sirens erected to alert citizens of impending doom could be seen throughout every major American city, ready to produce the most dreaded of sounds. Radio programming across the U.S. would frequently be interrupted to begin a testing of the emergency broadcast system, the listeners assured this was "only a test." In most cities large underground civil defense bunkers were constructed with the intent of saving as much of the local leadership and their families as possible, only to face the savage aftermath of nuclear destruction. Individual homeowners, if wealthy enough, constructed their own private underground bomb shelters, with a secure hatch necessary to keep out neighbors who improvidently were not prepared. Civil Defense brochures were readily available and provided the best advice possible for those not able to find shelter inside a "protected" facility, which included almost everyone. But everyone did know the standard procedure from Civil Defense. "When you hear the siren, enter a strong building and duck and cover. After the blast is over, stay inside and don't come out for several days waiting for the radiation to dissipate." That was the drill.

As the years progressed past that dangerous time, relations began to "normalize" between the United States and the Soviet Union. Perhaps a better description than normalize would be that although both nations despised what the other stood for, it was in the interest of both to never allow a situation to devolve to the extent that it had in the Fall of 1962. As a result of a thawing in the Cold War, there began a move away from Civil Defense, and by the 1980s it had become a shadow of its former self. Inherent in this move was the growing belief, peculiar to the political left, that it was useless anyway since the nation would be completely destroyed along with most of the world. The political left in America and Europe appeared to embrace another belief as well, that should the U.S. become too secure from nuclear attack through an effective system of protection, it might cause "warmongers" to start a nuclear war. Then in the early 1990s with the demise of the Soviet Union, the threat of nuclear annihilation appeared to recede into history and with it the last vestiges of Civil Defense in America.

The belief within the political left that any form of missile defense was destabilizing became a staple within its ranks, carried down over the years by its writers, politicians, and the rank and file. When, in January 2009, Barack Obama was sworn in as president, the aversion to Civil

Defense came with him to the White House. Once in office, Obama cut funding to the U.S. Missile Defense Agency airborne laser program. Mounted on a Boeing 747, the system was proving effective in shooting down ballistic missiles during their vulnerable launch phase. On February 11, 2010, it successfully shot down a sea-launched, liquid-fueled ballistic missile in the ignition stage within two minutes of launch. Then, only an hour later it downed a land launched solid-state rocket.[2] Not satisfied with cutting funds for a second airborne laser Boeing 747, Obama would scale back the ground-based anti-missile system scheduled to be built to defend against the Iranian and North Korean missiles. The dream that Ronald Reagan had of an America safe from missiles carrying nuclear destruction, and denigrated at the time of its announcement was finally a possibility. What Reagan could not dream of, however, was that a president many years later would scale back the fruition of years of research.

In line with the political left's missile defense reasoning, Obama would reverse a deal worked out by the Bush Administration, with the assistance of the brave Poles, to erect a system of missile protection for Europe based in Poland.[3] From the perspective of the left, the perceived threat posed to the world by such civil defense efforts was now being scaled back.

But then something strange happened. Occasionally, it is possible to glean a peek into what is really going on at the highest levels of government, even though access to documents classified as "TOP SECRET" are not available for casual eyes. And so it is with developments on the Civil Defense front in America.

In December 2010, an unusual article appeared in the *New York Times* titled "U.S. Rethinks Strategy for the Unthinkable." Within the article it was revealed that the Obama Administration was beginning to ramp up Civil Defense efforts specifically against a nuclear detonation within a U.S. city. This abrupt change of heart pertaining to Civil Defense did not apparently include reversing the recently downgraded, yet effective methods of dealing with nuclear missiles from rogue nations such as North Korea and Iran. Apparently, that was not an area of danger being addressed by administration officials. The new effort appears to be a substantial one, taking the nation back to a time many thought would never return. W. Craig Fugate, administrator of the Federal Emergency Management Agency (FEMA), in an effort to explain the sudden interest in Civil Defense said in an interview with the *Times*, "We have to get past the mental block that says it's too terrible to think about. We have to be ready to deal with it." Continuing, he pointed out that people needed to learn how to "best protect themselves."

The article went on to say that the administration is, "...moving aggressively to conduct drills, prepare communication guides, and raise awareness among emergency planners of how to educate the public." In an almost Dr. Strangelove sense, the administration is suddenly making the case that a nuclear detonation is "potentially survivable for thousands, especially with adequate shelter and education." Their concern appears to center on the belief that in such an event, citizens will instinctively attempt to run for some familiar place, be it home or the work place, and, in so doing, unnecessarily expose themselves to more radiation.[4]

In June 2010, administration officials released a 130-page unclassified planning guide to emergency officials around the nation. The guide explained how to respond to a nuclear attack, stressing citizen awareness and education prior to any attack as the top priority. For an administration that has cut funding for protection against missiles from rogue nations, its problem is how to spread the word without seeming alarmist, indicated the *Times*. But the director of the National Center for Disaster Preparedness at Columbia University worried that, "There is no penetration of the message coming out of the federal government." He went on to say, "It's deeply frustrating that we seem unable to bridge the gap between the new insights and using them to inform the public." Those "new insights" appeared to be the notion that a nuclear detonation is surviv-able, if certain steps are taken by those in the impacted area. What the *New York Times* article did not explain was why after over 40 years the U.S. was suddenly pressing to reconstruct the old Civil Defense program.

* * * * * * *

On April 12, 2010, the headline in *The Sunday Times* said it all, "Hill-ary Clinton fears al-Qaeda is obtaining nuclear weapons material." As secretary of state, she had taken office a little over a year earlier and was now speaking on the eve of a nuclear summit in Washington dedicated to stopping the growing danger of terrorist organizations, like al-Qaeda, from obtaining a nuclear weapon. At the summit were leaders from 47 nations, representing a gathering of national leaders only exceeded by those gath-ered at the founding of the United Nations in 1945. For the new president, Barack Obama, and his secretary of state, the summit was the result of the growing threat posed by the possibility of nuclear weapons falling into the hands of terrorists. White House deputy national security advisor Ben Rhodes summed up the reason for the grand gathering of world leaders:

> We know that terrorists groups, including al-Qaeda, are pursu-ing the materials to build a nuclear weapon and we know that they have the intent to use one [which would be] a catastrophic danger to American national security and to global security were they able to carry out that kind of attack.[6]

Rhodes' comments appeared to sum up the growing concerns of leaders across the globe, that an organization of fanatics will obtain and use a nuclear weapon on a major city. From all indications, al-Qaeda has been pursuing a working nuclear bomb as well as radioactive material to build one with the intention to use it.

But within the halls of power, rarely do the true thoughts of governments become exposed for all to see. Like playing cards in a high stakes poker game, private diplomatic conversations are kept close to the vest, secure from prying eyes. Conversations between governments and their diplomats are simply not revealed to the public. They are kept private so that all the players discussing a sensitive matter can speak freely, making progress possible. But the United States' cards in that diplomatic game began getting turned over by Wikileaks, able to be viewed by friend and foe alike for better or worse. In the age of Wikileaks, amazingly, U.S. diplomatic correspondence was able to be stolen and given to the rogue organization. With one embarrassing private diplomatic correspondence after another revealed, the U.S. State Department was busy doing damage control. But one particular Wikileaks release was especially disturbing.

The release related to al-Qaeda and nuclear weapons, producing the following headlines in various publications:

"Al-Qaeda on brink of using nuclear bomb" *Free Republic*[7]

"Wikileaks documents shows al-Qaeda has nuclear bomb" *Conservative Examiner*[8]

"Al-Qaeda on brink of using nuclear bomb" *Fox Nation*[9]

Within the released private diplomatic cables, a "leading atomic regulator" privately warned that the world stands on the brink of a "nuclear 9/11." The regulator is not named, but there is an indication within the cable that this person is at the top of his profession. The private diplomatic cable goes on to explain that al-Qaeda is on the verge of producing radioactive weapons, after having secured nuclear materials and having recruited rogue scientists.[10]

Others shared the government's pessimistic view expressed in the "private" diplomatic cable. Harvard professor Matthew Bunn has created a model that estimates the probability of a nuclear detonation in a major city over a 10-year period and reaches the conclusion that the odds are

29%. But his is one of the more optimistic estimates. Richard Garwin, a designer of the hydrogen bomb, told a congressional committee in March 2007, that he estimated a "20 percent per year probability" of a nuclear explosion in a U.S. or European city. Garwin is no average scientist. It was he that Nobel laureate physicist Enrico Fermi called, "...the only true genius I had ever met." Warren Buffet, one of the world's wealthiest persons and famous odds maker in pricing insurance, has concluded that nuclear terrorism is "inevitable," adding, "I don't see any way it won't happen."[11]

Graham Allison, writing in *Technology Review* in an article titled, "Nuclear Deterrence in the Age of Nuclear Terrorism" states, "No one who has examined the evidence has any doubt that al-Qaeda is deadly serious about exploding a nuclear bomb." Former CIA Director George Tenet, in charge of the agency at the time of 9/11, states in his memoir:

> The most senior leaders of al-Qaeda are still singularly focused on acquiring WMD...The main threat is the nuclear one. I am convinced that this is where Osama bin Laden and his operatives desperately want to go.[12]

It has indeed become clear that al-Qaeda wants to acquire nuclear bombs, with the intention of actually using them. It is also clear that in order to accomplish that goal the terrorist organization has two basic options. The first option is to acquire a fully operational bomb on the black market. The second option is to acquire fissile material for the construction of one. So just how difficult is it to build a nuclear bomb? Consider the following story from 1964.

With the Cuban Missile crisis having taken place only two years earlier, the Pentagon began considering the nature of nuclear proliferation and how easy it would be for some unknown nation to develop nuclear weapons. As a result, the "Nth country" project was initiated. The goal was to see if two post graduates in physics could, without any classified documentation to help them, build a workable nuclear bomb design.

Having access to only public domain information, essentially the library, they went about trying to build the bomb. After 30 months of labor they submitted the design to the Livermore Laboratory. About two weeks later the general in charge of the project announced to the duo the results. They had, in fact, developed a set of design plans that, if followed, would create a workable atom bomb about the size of the one dropped on Hiroshima in 1945. Ominously, that success was based off of information accessible in 1964. However, since that time much more has been published in the public domain concerning the subject, leaving considerably more information for a potential A-bomb builder.[13]

* * * * * * *

Perhaps the most disturbing reports came to the attention of U.S. officials in late 2001, shortly after the attacks on 9/11, from United Press International terrorism correspondent Richard Sale. The borders of Israel are, perhaps, the most secure in the world, with security officials refining their techniques and systems over the course of decades to stop deadly terrorist's attacks against their citizens. As such it was no surprise that in October 2001, when a Muslim driving a Volkswagen mini-bus tried entering the country through the Allenby Bridge located between Jordan and Israel, it was stopped and searched. What the superbly trained Israeli border guards found would cause sleepless nights across the world, but especially within Israel and the United States. The driver, a Pakistani who, it was later discovered had ties to al-Qaeda, was asked to step out of the bus. Within the rear of the vehicle was a rucksack weighing about 70 pounds. When asked what the contents of it were, he smiled and responded that it was only computer equipment. However, the Israelis are trained to profile potential terrorists; and that training appears to have saved many lives on that day. One of the soldiers opened the rucksack and discovered a bomb of some type.[14] [15]

After closer inspection, the bomb appeared to be a radiological explosive device, perhaps a dirty bomb designed to spread radioactivity, and so it was quickly delivered to the Mossad for further inspection. Shockingly, the device was not a dirty bomb, but a fully functional nuclear bomb. Adding to the concern of all, it was not a homemade nuclear bomb constructed after acquiring highly enriched uranium, but a sophisticated plutonium-implosion devise that had been developed by the KGB.[16][17]

Since the driver was a Pakistani, the Israelis contacted Pakistan's intelligence service seeking assistance in finding his accomplices. A few weeks later several suspects were taken into custody. What one of them had to say would send chills down the spine of U.S. officials. He would indicate that al-Qaeda had successfully smuggled two fully functional nuclear weapons into the United States. The UPI report would add the following, ominous detail:

> "What was disconcerting about the (suspect's) information was that he knew details of the activation of the weapons and their construction that are not in the public domain," the U.S. expert analyst said.... It could be a nuclear backpack weapon "or some other Russian portable nuclear weapon," he said.[18][19]

Rep. Chris Shays, R-Conn., Chairman of the House Committee on national security, commenting on the possibility that al-Qaeda might already have nuclear weapons within the United States, indicated "It's possible, and it's very scary." Shays would add the following:

> We know that bin Laden made strenuous efforts to buy these weapons, we know that security at some Russian nuclear arsenals was terrible, we know that some Russian officials were corrupt. We are told of attempted thefts and of lots of plots that were foiled, but we are never told of the plots that succeeded.[20][21]

Peter Probst, formerly of the Pentagon's Office of Assistant Secretary of Defense for Special Operations and Low Intensity Conflict, would put it this way, "It would seem probable that some (bin Laden) deals for purchasing (nuclear) weapons did go through." An unnamed former CIA official in the UPI report discussing Russian nuclear backpacks added, "It's not a big reach at all to say that it's probable that bin Laden has been able to obtain this system."[22][23]

The following report from the Lebanese magazine *Al-Watan Al-'Arabi* might explain where al-Qaeda could have secured such ready-to-use nuclear weapons. On November 13, 1998 in Nicosia, Cyprus, the Foreign Broadcast Information Service (FBIS) picked up the following transmission from an unidentified *Al-Watan* correspondent in Moscow. It indicated that a senior western terrorism expert informed the correspondent that all of the world's intelligence agencies were focusing on a grave (nuclear) threat against their nations, something that far exceeded any terrorist act up to that time. In other words, they possessed information that led them to believe al-Qaeda had obtained nuclear weapons. According to the information that was gathered shortly before the report, al-Qaeda bought nuclear weapons that had been smuggled out of the former Soviet Union. According to the source, it is known that bin Laden paid $30 million and two tons of refined heroin with a street value of $70 million for 20 small nuclear weapons that came from several republics in the region, including Ukraine, Kazakhstan, Turkmenistan, and Russia. Along with the deal, it was reported, came a number of nuclear technicians to keep the systems in proper working order.[24]

* * * * * * *

It appears from the UPI report that it is possible al-Qaeda has obtained some unspecified number of small and very portable nuclear weapons. But if this is the case, it raises a legitimate question. Why haven't they used them? For that matter, why has there not been any major attack on American soil since 9/11? There are several possibilities. One is that they simply do not possess nuclear weapons, in spite of a significant amount of smoke indicating a nuclear threat exists. Or, perhaps, they have had trouble bringing the weapons into the country. However, considering the porous nature of the borders, that is unlikely. The other possibility is that they possess them, and have smuggled them into the United States. If that is true, then why have they delayed using them?

What might answer that question is a rumor, one reportedly to have made the rounds in the Washington Beltway during the Bush Administration in the aftermath of 9/11. It is said that following the 9/11 attacks, and the subsequent threat of New York being nuked, someone from the Bush Administration got word back to al-Qaeda that should the U.S. be nuked, Mecca would be next. The rationale behind such a threat is that since terrorists show little regard for their own lives, it is necessary to threaten something that does have meaning to them. One U.S. Congressman, Tom Tancredo, has openly stated that in his opinion, that counter-threat is how to handle the threat from al-Qaeda.[25][26] Whether or not such a threat was used to protect America from another attack is open to question. But this we do know, that only three months after the 9/11 attacks, the Bush Administration issued a nuclear policy statement indicating that the U.S. reserves the right to use nuclear weapons "to deter a wide range of threats..."[27] Then on February 8, 2008, Bush National Security Advisor Stephen Hadley announced the following change to U.S nuclear policy, stating that the United States had recently adopted "a new declaratory policy to help deter terrorists from using weapons of mass destruction against the United States, our friends, and allies." Hadley went on to indicate that this policy would threaten with retaliation "those states, organizations, or individuals who might enable or facilitate terrorists in obtaining or using weapons of mass destruction."[28] The article, appropriately titled "The New Deterrence," noted a change that was directed to terrorist groups such as al-Qaeda and the nations and/or organizations that assist them. The change essentially created the prospect of nuclear annihilation against a nation that did not directly launch the attack, but in the opinion of the U.S. was somehow involved. Thus, U.S. policy now enabled a retaliatory strike against a nation not overtly involved in an attack against America. The open acknowledgment of such a policy did, in a vague way, appear to open the door to the type of strike alluded to in the Beltway rumor.

With al-Qaeda possibly finding success in their 15 year quest for nuclear weapons, and with the Mexican border wide open during that time frame, the threat that nuclear weapons have already been smuggled into the U.S. has to be considered legitimate. If, in fact, that has happened, then one of the last lines of defense against catastrophe is to use whatever interrogation methods are necessary to extract information from captured al-Qaeda operatives. No doubt, some operatives possess information that can lead to others within their organization that might be involved in the group's nuclear effort, maybe even a nuclear cell within America.

However, during the Obama Administration significant "change" has come to U.S. counter-terrorism policy. That change is probably best described by an April 2011 *Los Angeles Times* article titled, "CIA has slashed its terrorism role."

> He's considered one of world's most dangerous terrorism suspects, and the U.S. offered a $1-million reward for his capture in 2005. Intelligence experts say he's a master bomb maker and extremist leader who possesses a wealth of information about Al Qaeda-linked groups in Southeast Asia. Yet the U.S. has made no move to interrogate or seek custody of Indonesian militant Umar Patek since he was apprehended this year by officials in Pakistan with the help of a CIA tip, U.S. and Pakistani officials say.

> The little-known case highlights a sharp difference between President Obama's counter-terrorism policy and that of his predecessor, George W. Bush. Under Obama, the CIA has

killed more people than it has captured, mainly through drone missile strikes in Pakistan's tribal areas. At the same time, it has stopped trying to detain or interrogate suspects caught abroad, except those captured in Iraq and Afghanistan.

"The CIA is out of the detention and interrogation business," said a U.S. official who is familiar with intelligence operations but was not authorized to speak publicly.[29]

The shift within the Obama Administration away from interrogations has been a tectonic one in the war against al-Qaeda. Additionally, although it is commendable to kill as many al-Qaeda operatives as possible, capturing them for interrogation purposes could be dramatically more beneficial. Since the real way to protect the American homeland is to gather as much information as possible on the terrorist organization's operations within the U.S., capturing al-Qaeda members is often more beneficial than killing them. But dead men tell no tales, and in the cases where those killed could have been captured, resulting in a potential treasure trove of information, that opportunity has been lost forever. The apparent ideological justification for this policy change away from interrogations to actually killing them is that U.S. interrogation methods are harsh.

Continuing to fulfill his campaign promise of "change," Obama also altered U.S. policy concerning the use of nuclear weapons, reversing the subtle threat inherent in Bush's 2008 new policy. In an April 5, 2010 *New York Times* article it was noted:

It eliminates much of the ambiguity that has deliberately existed in American nuclear policy since the opening days of the cold war. For the first time, the United States is explicitly committing not to use nuclear weapons against nonnuclear states that are in compliance with the Nuclear Nonproliferation Treaty...[30]

The *Times* article went on to point out that "Mr. Obama's strategy is a sharp shift from those of his predecessors." And so it was, especially by specifically removing the intentional ambiguity always contained within America's nuclear policy so adversaries would be relegated to a dangerous nuclear guessing game of what would happen if they nuked America. Indeed it was a sharp shift with even the title of the article saying it all, "Obama Limits When U.S. Would Use Nuclear Arms." The new policy made it clear that if there ever was any vague threat against Mecca, in some nuclear quid-pro-quo standoff, it was now gone.

CHAPTER SIXTEEN

What Is Next?

I n days of yore when man's grandest adventures began from towns near the sea, great ships would depart their docks to ply the oceans for lands far away, in the hope of adventure, land, and wealth. Harbor workers bitten with wander lust would remain on the dock, relegated to watching as the ships they had just filled with supplies would silently slip out of harbor, left only with their imaginations of what adventures await-ed those on board. Long ago on one such day from a port in southern Spain, dock workers watched as three great ships lumbered slowly out of harbor, able to hear orders shouted by the masters of the vessels to those that labored to keep their great sails open. Soon, all that would remain of the proud vessels were their dimming images on the horizon. Watching the last of the ships disappear into a blending of sky and sea, those watch-ing would return to the drudgery of their labors, back to the dock.

Those three ships had set sail for a land thought to exist somewhere far to the east, far beyond where any sailors had dared go before them. But this adventure would truly alter the course of world history, expand-ing the map of the old world to include the new. The land they would discover was destined to become a safe haven for people across the globe, eventually becoming a God-fearing people whose nation would grow and prosper over the centuries surpassing Europe. In that same year, 1492, King Ferdinand and Queen Isabella of Spain embarked on another grand move, but one far less admirable than the discovery of the new continent. As Columbus was sailing into history, back in Spain the royalty was expelling all the Jews from the country, removing them from a safe haven they had known for centuries. But as one safe haven ended, another began opening in the newly discovered land so far away from the pogroms of Europe.

Every age has its great adventures and with modern man it is space exploration that reaches into the new frontier. The brave explorers in their shiny suits streaking toward the heavens in the space shuttle, brought the explorers' spirit with them. From Central Florida people viewed the twin fires south of Cape Canaveral lighting up the sky, marking a beginning as well as an end. Since the Wright brothers lifted man off the ground, many great adventures have come from the air. But it is also from the sky that two days of infamy have visited America, December 7, 1941, and September 11, 2001, both marking the beginning of war. Big events in the history of America and the world often happen when they are least expected, ushering in a new age. It is from that perspective that we seek to answer the question asked in the beginning of the book. If these are the foretold *times*, then what is next?

* * * * * * *

The restoration of Israel as a nation in 1948 represented the most important Biblical event in almost two thousand years. What many scholars across the centuries could not accept as a literal prophecy of that nation resurrecting back to life again after almost two thousand years of being *scattered*, unfolded just as the ancient words assured the reader they would. However, the Jewish rebirth in the land of their ancestors was not an easy one. Surrounded by hostile nations dedicated to killing the baby state, the Jews would have to fight against odds that would scare any gambler. But in spite of the large armies arrayed to prevent the old prophecies from coming to pass, the incredible odds were overcome with Israel winning her independence and fulfilling all that was foretold. In the years that followed, a multitude of hostile Arabs appeared to dedicate their national existence to destroying the peaceful new state, ignoring the legal status granted it by the United Nations. They would fail in their attempts in 1967, and again in 1973, to "drive the Jews into the sea." Ironically, those subsequent efforts would result in even more of the Promised Land falling into the hands of those the ancient words promised would attain it.

Having failed to destroy the small Jewish state by force of arms, the enemies surrounding her would change tactics, organizing into terrorist organizations dedicated to targeting the lives of Israeli civilians, especially the children. They would also embrace the United Nations, whose original resolution they had despised, seeking that institution to impose a settlement along borders that would make Israel only nine miles wide at its narrowest point, vulnerable once again to being divided in a future war. But, in 2011, the division of Israel would not take the armies of Allah to accomplish, instead it would be proposed by an American president as part of a "peace" settlement, breaking with presidents since Truman that instinctively protected the Jews from a potential second Holocaust. But the Divine has a way of protecting that which He has created, with warnings emanating from nature as the efforts against the land continued, increasing in both their frequency and severity.

At the conclusion of *The Israel Omen* it was speculated upon if the "coincidence" of disasters relative to the diplomatic efforts against the land would continue or if they would simply cease, calling into question the entire thesis of that book. However, since that writing three more "coincidences" have taken place in as many years, adding their weight to the concept of Divine intervention on behalf of the restored Israel. But these are strange happenings these "coincidences," things the likes of which have not been seen in two thousand years, since the time when Jesus walked the Earth and miracles ran rampant, staggering all that watched. Just like that time long ago, the current strange events appear to have a much greater meaning.

If these events constitute a warning from the Divine against mankind's efforts to reverse His ancient promise of a restored Israel within the restored lands of her ancestors, then the common message contained within each creates a frightening potential. That message appears to strike an unmistakable cord and one repeated over and over again, a litany of the same message since 1991, the year efforts against the restored land began. The message, peace...then sudden destruction carries the potential that a cataclysm that is foreshadowing event is approaching.

With the very old words of the prophet Zechariah appearing to come to life in this age with the advent of the international group referred to as the Quartet (*four horns*), the notion that unusual times have begun to unfold is gathering steam. Based on current news reports, this group of *four horns* is leading the effort to declare a Palestinian state within the United Nations. But based on Zechariah's writings, this, too, would be expected. Also, based on his writings, some grand removal of the land should take place, requiring a promised response by the Biblical *carpenters* we are assured will be sent to *fray* the nations. In fact, there is every reason to believe that two acts of fraying by the *carpenters* have already taken place.

The latest effort by the Obama Administration against the land ignores the promises of several previous American presidents, reassuring the modern Israelites they would never again have to be vulnerable to destruction. This may explain why some of the president's biggest supporters have been critical of his plan, and apparently explains the departure of the statesman George Mitchell. No one is quite sure why the administration felt the need to announce its new policy in Washington just prior to the arrival of the Israeli prime minister there, but one thing is certain. The new U.S. policy is one that essentially takes the Palestinian position, and is a drastic departure from policies followed by a long line of presidents. It is also a policy that runs hard against the promise of the land from God to the Jews.

In the beginning of this book, a challenge was presented to those that believe the long awaited *times* foretold by the prophets have finally arrived. That challenge was two-fold. How could the dreaded coming world leader, expected to be a 900-pound gorilla, enter a world stage already occupied by another 900-pound gorilla, America? And secondly, how could the holy Jewish Temple become rebuilt on the Temple Mount? Both would appear only possible in a radically altered world than the one currently in place. Concerning that possibility, this is what we know.

The efforts by al-Qaeda have been methodical and widespread in attempting to secure small nuclear weapons. We also know from the UPI report that they may have been successful. We know that al-Qaeda views Israel as the "little Satan" and the United States as the "big Satan," implying that the United States is a more important target. We also know that the nuclear bomb attempted to be smuggled into Israel was spotted because the Israelis have excellent border security. We can assume that al-Qaeda has an even greater desire to detonate one within the United States. We know that the borders of the United States are highly vulnerable to penetration. We can, therefore, believe that if al-Qaeda attempted to smuggle a nuke into Israel, viewed by them as the lesser of their two Satans, they have also attempted to do so with the United States. Since the U.S. borders have been virtually unprotected for two decades, it is highly likely they have succeeded in smuggling into the U.S. whatever they wanted. You be the judge if the above, cold logic is reasonable.

These things we also know. We know that within the Bible is a prophecy telling the world that the nation of Israel would come back into existence again after being *scattered* among the nations. We know that amazing event happened almost two thousand years after the scattering. We know that the Bible is filled with promises from God indicating that the lands currently occupied by Israel are lands He has granted them a deed to forever. The Scriptures saying this are quite numerous. We know that, in 1991, the United States began an effort, diplomatically, to remove the Promised Lands effectively reversing those promises of God. However, since that time there have occurred, often to the day, at least 13 historically severe disasters "coincidental" to those efforts. We also know that the international group called the Quartet (*four horns*) appears to fulfill a specific prophecy given by Zechariah that has a clear warning associated with it. We know that the first two gatherings of this group experienced historically severe catastrophes coinciding with their efforts. Based on the old prophecy, such catastrophes should have been expected. We also know from news reports that the Quartet (*four horns*) is a leading factor in the United Nations' vote to declare a Palestinian state. Again, this, too, would be expected from the prophecy.

We know that the diplomatic efforts in question have a common theme behind them of *peace*. We know that the historically severe disasters associated with those diplomatic efforts have *destruction* as a common denominator. We also know that the *destruction* took place immediately coinciding with those efforts, usually within one day, making them quite *sudden* on the heels of the *peace* efforts. This creates a recurring theme since 1991 of *peace...then sudden destruction; peace...then sudden destruction*. We know that such words specifically fit a prophetic warning in 1 Thessalonians quite well. However, it is important to note that the warning in that passage appears to be referring to an event that will come deep into the *times*, so the real question is if what appear to be continuous Divine warnings since 1991 are alerting the world that possibly a foreshadowing type of event is approaching. Then there is another form of logic to consider. Because these warnings have been on a historical level, the end result should bring about an event several magnitudes worse. But here, too, perhaps, we are given some indication of what is coming. Since the recurring theme of *peace...then sudden destruction* may in fact be pointing to a form of foreshadowing event of another, much larger event approaching, then the other scripture relating to it in 2 Peter appears to describe the approaching cataclysm with a detailed description of what resembles a nuclear detonation. So, what might bring forth such a dire conclusion to this multitude of warnings given to mankind since 1991?

The creation of a Palestinian state by the U.N/Quartet or otherwise in the midst of the restored land of Israel should bring cataclysm if the thesis of this book is correct. The timing of such an event would probably be related to the completion of removing Israeli control over the area given to the Palestinians, the removal of troops, etc., with an official declaration that it is finished. This would match what happened after Gaza was removed. It was only on the day the removal from Gaza was declared officially completed by Israel, that Hurricane Katrina popped up, noticed for the first time by the national hurricane center, not before. On the other hand, if Israel refuses the dictates of the world body in a "world verses Israel scenario," then, perhaps, "only" a historically severe disaster that is global will befall the nations lined up against the Holy Land. The above is speculation based on previous happenings, but, truly, only God knows exactly what will happen, if anything, and when. It is left to the Believer to be *sober*. In the first instance where Israel complies with a plan that creates a Palestinian state, there will be grand proclamations of *peace* heard worldwide. If what is written herein is correct, then in that circumstance what the Believer should look for is *when they say peace*.

TO THE LOGICAL MIND

The litany of events catalogued within
The Israel Omen testifies to the supernatural nature of
the Bible. And if supernatural, then it is a message from
the Divine. If a message from the Divine, then it is of
the greatest importance to the individual. Therefore,
since it directs the individual to the Son of God
as their only eternal hope, then...

REFERENCES

CHAPTER TWO

1. *Holy Bible*, King James Version, Book of Zechariah; Chapter 1

CHAPTER THREE

2. "The Romans Destroy the Temple at Jerusalem, 70 AD," *EyeWitness to History*, www.eyewitnesstohistory.com

3. *Holy Bible*, King James Version, Book of Exodus

4. *Holy Bible*, King James Version, Book of Deuteronomy

5. *Holy Bible*, King James Version, Book of Judges

6. *Holy Bible*, King James Version, Book of Jeremiah

7. *Holy Bible*, King James Version, Book of Ezekiel

8. *Holy Bible*, King James Version, Book of Mark

9. *Holy Bible*, King James Version, Book of Isaiah

CHAPTER FOUR

1. Wikipedia, Deepwater Horizon, Accessed June 16, 2010 http://en.wikipedia.org/wiki/Deepwater_Horizon

2. CNN.com, "Clinton: Israel settlement announcement insulting," March 12, 2010, http://www.cnn.com/2010/WORLD/meast/03/12/israel.clinton/index.html

3. Roger Cohen, *The New York Times*, "Beating the Mideast's Black Hole," April 27, 2010, http://www.nytimes.com/2010/04/27/opinion/27iht-edcohen.html

4. Ibid.

5. Henry Fountain, Tom Zeller, Jr., *The New York Times*, "Panel Suggests Signs of Trouble Before Rig Explosion," Accessed June 11, 2010 May 25, 2010, http://www.nytimes.com/2010/05/26/us/26rig.html?pagewanted=print

6. David Hammer, *The Times Picayune*, "Oil spill hearings: BP man on Deepwater Horizon rig refuses to testify, says he will take the Fifth" http://www.nola.com/news/gulf-oil-spill/index.ssf/2010/05/oil_spill_hearings_bp_man_on_d.html

7. Sharyl Attkisson, CBS News, "Oil Rig Explosion Followed Argument, Warning" May 26, 2010, http://www.cbsnews.com/stories/2010/05/26/eveningnew/main6521981.shtml Accessed June 11, 2010

8. David Brennan, *The Israel Omen*, Teknon Publishing

9. *The Independent* "Netanyahu raises stakes with US over settlements in East Jerusalem"

10. David Hammer, *The Times Picayune*, "Oil spill hearings: BP man on Deepwater Horizon rig refuses to testify, says he will take the Fifth" http://www.nola.com/news/gulf-oil-spill/index.ssf/2010/05/oil_spill_hearings_bp_man_on_d.html

11. Ibid.

12. *ABC News, Associated Press* "Israeli PM rejects calls for east Jerusalem freeze as US envoy launches new peace mission"

13. Wikipedia, "Shas" http://en.wikipedia.org/wiki/Shas

14. *The Christian Science Monitor,* Is Israel willing to freeze East Jerusalem construction?, April 22, 2010, Ilene Prusher, Staff Writer

15. Fox News.com, Associated Press, "Signs of progress as Obama envoy wraps up mission," April 25, 2010, http://www.foxnews.com/world/2010/04/25/aides-abbas-meet-obama-soon-date-set/print

16. CNN, "Official: 'Direct order' against building in East Jerusalem", April 26, 2010, http://news.blogs.cnn.com/2010/04/26/councilman-direct-order-against-building-in-east-jerusalem/

17. Henry Fountain, Tom Zeller, Jr., *The New York Times*, "Panel Suggests Signs of Trouble Before Rig Explosion," Accessed June 11, 2010 May 25, 2010, http://www.nytimes.com/2010/05/26/us/26rig.html?pagewanted=print

18. Ibid.

19. Ibid.

20. Steven Hurst, Associated Press, "Analysis: Obama's Mideast diplomacy sees gains" April 27, 2010 www.newsvine.com/_news2010/04/27/4209625-analysis-obamas-mideast-diplomacy-sees-gains Accessed June 11, 2010

21. Amy Teibel, Associated Press, *AP News Break*: Israel halts east Jerusalem building" April 27, 2010 http://abcnews.go.com/International/wireStory?id=10473798 Accessed June 11, 2010

22. CNN, "Official: 'Direct order' against building in East Jerusalem", April 26, 2010, http://news.blogs.cnn.com/2010/04/26/councilman-direct-order-against-building-in-east-jerusalem/

23. Amy Teibel, Associated Press, *AP News Break*: Israel halts east Jerusalem building" April 27, 2010 http://abcnews.go.com/International/wireStory?id=10473798 Accessed June 11, 2010

24. BBC, US push to renew Mid-East talks," April 23, 2010, http://news.bbc.co.uk/2/hi/2/middle_east/8639470.stm Accessed June 11, 2010

25. David Hammer, *The Times Picayune*, "Oil spill hearings: Dramatic testimony of the rig's final moments" May 28, 2010, www.nola.com/news/gulf-oil-splii/index.ssf/2010/05/oil_spill_hearings_dramatic_te.html Accessed June 11, 2010

26. Ibid.

27. Josh Harkinson, *Mother Jones*, "The rig's on fire! I told you this was going to happen!" June 7, 2010, http://motherjones.com/blue-marble/2010/06/rigs-fire-i-told-you-was-gonna-happen   Accessed June 11, 2010

CHAPTER FIVE

1. Jerusalem – The Old City, Jewish Virtual Library, http://www.
   jewishvirtuallibrary.org/jsource/vie/Jerusalem2.html

2. Ibid.

3. Advertising Standards Authority, United Kingdom, http://www.asa.org.uk/

4. Ibid.

CHAPTER SIX

1. Wikipedia, George J. Mitchell, http://en.wikipedia.org/wiki/George_J._
   Mitchell

2. Mortimer Zuckerman, *The Wall Street Journal*, "Obama's Jerusalem Stonewall:
   Demanding a Construction Freeze Reverses Decades of U.S. Policy," April 27,
   2010, http://eyeonfreedom.com/index.php/obamas-jerusalem-stonewall-
   demanding-a-construction-freeze-reverses-decades-of-u-s-policy/

3. *Pajamas Media*, "Obama's Obsessional Focus on 'Settlements'" http://
   pajamasmedia.com/tatler/2011/06/22/obamas-obsessional-focus-on-
   settlements/

4. Stephen M. Walt, *The Washington Post*, "Will Obama Settle for Failure in
   the Middle East?," September 20, 2009, http://www.washingtonpost.com/
   wp-dyn/content/article/2009/09/18/AR2009091801146.html

5. Tony Karon, *Time*, "Stalemate Looms in Obama's Mideast
   Peace Effort," November 03, 2009, http://www.time.com/time/
   printout/0,8816,1934119,00.html

6. Caroline Glick, *The Jerusalem Post*, "Obama's Abandonment of America," http://
   www.carolineglick.com/e/2011/05/obamas-abandonment-of-america.php

7. FrontpageMag.com, "Whitewashing the Muslim Brotherhood – The
   Failure of American Middle East Studies Professors," hppt://www.
   prophecynews watch.com/2011/May18/1861.html

8. Ibid.

9. Poll: Most Egyptians favor annulling peace with Israel, *Jerusalem Post*, http://www.prophecynewswatch.com/2011/April22/2221.html

10. Associated Press, Egypt's Muslim Brotherhood Condemns Bin Laden Killing," May 2, 2011, http://www.foxnews.com/world/2011/05/02/egypts-muslim-brotherhood-condemns-bin-laden-killing/

11. Chris Rovsar, *New York Magazine*, "Saudi King Abdullah to Obama: Don't Humiliate' Mubarak," 02/10/2011, http://nymag.com/daily/intel/2011/02/saudi_king_abdullah_to_obama_d.html

12. Susan Jones, *Conservative Underground*, Saudis Turn to China, Russia, April 7, 2011, http://www.conservativeunderground.com/forum505/showthread.php?t=38721

13. Helene Cooper & Mark Landler, *The New York Times*, Saudi and Iranian Interests create Middle East diplomacy dilemma, March 18, 2011, http://tech.mit.edu/V131/N14/wire2.html

14. Mark Lavie, Associated Press, "Egypt to open Rafah crossing permanently," May 25, 2011, http://newsyahoo.com/s/ap/20110525/ap_on_re_mi_ea/ml_egypt_gaza_border/print

15. Caroline Glick, Obama's Newest Ambush, *Jerusalem Post*, May 17, 2011, http://www.jpost.com/Opinion/Columnists/Article.aspx?id=220307

16. Ibid.

17. Ibid.

18. Ibid.

19. Jonathon Seidl, *The Blaze*, "Hamas Cleric: The Jews will be annihilated & Palestine will be capital of new Caliphate," http://www.theblaze.com/stories/hamas-cleric-the-jews-will-be-annihilated-palestine-will-be-capital-of-new-caliphate/

Chapter Seven

1. Mitchell Bard, The Six-Day War, Jewish Virtual Library, http://www.jewishvirtuallibrary.org/jsource/history/67_war.html

2. Ibid.

3. Ibid.

4. Ibid.

5. Ibid.

6. Ibid.

7. Fox News, "Muslim Brotherhood Members to Attend Obama's Cairo Speech," June 3, 2009, http://www.foxnews.com/politics/2009/06/03/muslim-brotherhood-members-attend-obamas-cairo-speech/

8. Pierre Tristam, *Middle East Issues*, "The Assissination of Egypt's Anwar Sadat" http://middleeast.about.com/od/egypt/a/me081006a.htm?p=1

9. Nile Gardner, *Daily Telegraph Blog*, "The Muslim Brotherhood gets a makeover from the Obama administration," http://blogs.telegraph.co.uk/news/nilegardiner/100075628/the-muslim-brotherhood-gets-a-pr-makeover-%E2%80%93from-the-us-director-of-national-intelligence/

10. Ibid.

11. Matt Spetainick, Reuters News, "Obama urges Egyptian army to ensure democratic change," February 11, 2011, http://www.reuters.com/assets/print?aid=USTRE71175920110211

12. Ibid.

13. Nile Gardner, *Daily Telegraph Blog*, "The Muslim Brotherhood gets a makeover from the Obama administration," http://blogs.telegraph.co.uk/news/nilegardiner/100075628/the-muslim-brotherhood-gets-a-pr-makeover-%E2%80%93from-the-us-director-of-national-intelligence/

14. Ibid.

CHAPTER EIGHT

1. *USA Today*, "Arabs may ask U.N. to recognize Palestinian state," October 15, 2010, http://www.usatoday.com/news/world/2010-10-15-un-palestinian-state_N.htm

2. Palestine-Mandate, Archive for the Palestine Category, April 30, 2011, http://palestine-mandate.com/catagory/palestine

3. Ibid.

4. *Jerusalem Post*, "Indyk: UN likely to vote in favor of Palestinian state," April 21, 2011, http://www.jpost.com/LandedPages/PrintArticle.aspx?id=217378

5. Aljazeera, "Sarkozy: France could recognize Palestine," May 4, 2011, http://english.aljazeera.net/news/middleeast/2011/05/201154155337666642.html

6. Tzvi Ben Gedalyahu, *Israeli National News*, April 27, 2011 Issue

7. Hillel Fendel, *Israeli National News*, May 5, 2011 Issue

8. *ChristianPost.com*, Nakba Day clashes are a precursor to declaration of PA State in September," May 20, 2011, http://www.prophecynewswatch.com/2011?may18/1821.html

9. *Haaretz News*, "Palestinian PM: We'll form de-facto state by 2011," August 25, 2009, http://www.haaretz.com/news/palestinian-pm-we-ll-form-de-facto-state-by-2011-1.282641

10. Ibid.

11. U.N. News Service, "New UN report assesses progress on Palestinian State-building efforts," http://www.un.org/apps/news/printnewsAr.asp?nid=38092

12. NJDC.org, "2008 Jewish Vote for Obama Exceeds All Expectations," November 5, 2008, http://www.njdc.org/site/page/jewish_vote_for_obama_exceeds_all_expectations

13. Caroline Glick, *Jerusalem Post*, "Obama's Abandonment of America," http://www.carolineglick.com/e/2011/05/obamas-abandonment-of-america.php

14. Ibid.

15. Ibid.

16. Charles Krauthammer, *The Washington Post*, "What Obama Did to Israel," May 25, 2011, http://www.washingtonpost.com/opinions/what-obama-did-to-israel/2011/05/26/AGJfYJCH_story.html

17. Ibid.

18. Henry Reske & Kathleen Walter, *Newsmax*, "Dershowitz: Obama Torpedoed Peace Process," May 20, 2011, http://www.newsmax.com/printtemplate.aspx?nodeid+397146

19. Steven Myers, *The New York Times*, "Amid Impasse in Peace Negotiations, America's Chief Middle East Envoy Resigns," May 13, 2011

20. *News Essentials*, "Quartet Will Recognize Palestinian State," April 4, 2011, http://newsessentials.wordpress.com/2011/04/20/quartet-will-recognize-palestinian-state/

21. Mark Weiss, *Irish Times*, "Middle East quartet may recognize a Palestinian state if talks not renewed," http://irishtimes.com/newspaper/world/2011/0420/1224295067124_pf.html

CHAPTER NINE

1. www.TheSpacePlace.com, John Glenn – Project Mercury Friendship 7 space history, http://www.thespaceplace.com/history/mercury/mercury06.html

2. Laura Zuckerman, Reuters, "Snowmelt, rain worsen flooding in northern plains," May 30, 2011

3. MSNBC.com, "Minot flood breaks 1881 record, homes swamped," 6/24/2011 http://www.msnbc.msn.com/cleanprint/CleanPrint Proxy.aspx?unique=1308939257900

4. Laura Thackeray, *The Billings Gazette*, "2011 flooding compares to other historic deluges '78, '75" http://billingsgazette.com/news/state-and-regional/montana/article_b64fc028-1c1b-599e-bfe0-69fa33156eaa.html

5. Adrian Sainz & Matt Sedensky, www.Salon.com, "Historic flooding slams Memphis," http://www.salon.com/news/feature/2011/05/10/us_mississippi_river_flooding_1

6. Wikipedia, "2011 Mississippi River floods,"

7. Laura Gottesdiener, *Huffington Post*, "Mississippi River Flooding Reaching Historic Levels" http://www.huffingtonpost/2011/05/11/mississippi-flooding-river-historic_n_860835.html

8. EzineMark.com, Mississippi 2011 Historic Flood in Pictures," May 5, 2011, http://society.ezinemark.com/mississippi-2011-historic-flood-in-picture-7736bfc4ac21.html

9. Jacob Batte, Reuters, "Historic Vicksburg, Mississippi faces flood siege," May 16, 2011

10. cbsNews.com, "Massive intentional folding begins in Louisiana," http://www.cbsnews.com/stories/2011/05/14/national/main20062948.shtml

11. Wikipedia, "Tornadoes of 2011," http://en.wikipepia.org/wiki/Tornadoes_of_2011

12. Wikipedia, "List of United States tornadoes in April 2011," http://en.wikipedia.org/wiki/List_of_United_States_tornadoes_in_April_2011

13. Wikipedia, "April 14-16 2011 tornadoes outbreak," http://en.wikipedia.org/wiki/April_14%E2%80%9316,_2011_tornado_outbreak

14. Ibid.

15. Wikipedia, "April 25-28, 2011 tornado outbreak"

16. NOAAnews.noaa.gov/2011_tornado_inforation.html

17. National Oceanic and Atmospheric Administration, "State of the Climate National Overview April 2011"

18. King James Bible, Book of Zechariah, Chapter 12

CHAPTER TEN

1. David Brennan, *The Israel Omen*, (New Orleans, Teknon Publishing, 2009)

2. Matti Friedman, *The Washington Times*, "Comatose Ariel Sharon moved from hospital," November 12, 2010, http://www.washingtontimes.com/news/2010/nov/12/comatose-ariel-sharon-moved-home-hospital/

3. Bob Woodward, *State of Denial*, (New York: Simon & Schuster, 2006) pp. 76-78

4. Associated Press-MSNBC, "Ex-Bush aides: He didn't recover from Katrina," 12/30/2008 [accessed 02/08/2009] http://www.msnbc.msn.com/id/28433687/

5. Ibid.

6. Robert Pear, "Hurricane Andrew; Breakdown Seen in U.S. Storm Aid," *The New York Times*, August 29, 1992 [accessed 4/26/2009] www.nytimes. com/1992/08/29/us/hurricane-andrew-breakdown-seen-in-us-storm-aid.html

CHAPTER ELEVEN

1. David Brennan, *The Israel Omen*, (New Orleans: Teknon Publishing, 2009)

2. Ibid.

3. Ibid.

4. Ibid.

5. David Kaplin, "The Cost Since 911," *Newsweek*, http://www.usnews.com/ usnews/news/badguys/061025/the_cost_since_911_1.htm

6. *Live Science*, "Billion Dollar Disasters a Chronology of Events," January 31, 2004 http://www.livescience.com/114-billion-dollar-disasters-chronology-events.html

7. M. J. Fennessy and J. L. Kinter III, *Journal of Climate*, http://journals. ametsoc.org/doi/abs/10.1175/2011JCLI3523.1

8. Martin Wolk, "How Katrina's Costs are Adding up," MSNBC.com, http:// www.msnbc.msn.com/id/9329293/ns/business-eye_on_the_economy/t/ how-hurricane-katrinas-costs-are-adding/

9. Edmund Conway, *The Telegraph*, "IMF puts total cost of crisis at $10.2 trillion, August 8, 2009, http://www.telegraph.co.uk/finance/ newsbysector/banksandfinance/5995810/IMF-puts-total-cost-of-crisis-at-7.1-trillion.html

10. Reuters, "Timeline: Gulf of Mexico oil spill," January 11. 2011, http:// www.reuters.com/article/2011/01/11/oilspill-bp-commission-idUSN1114564120110111

11. Birmingham *Business Journal*, http://www.bizjournals.com/birmingham/ print-edition/2011/05/13/storm-costs-could-reach-4-billion.html

12. Newsmax.com, "Tornadoes' Cost $7 Billion in One May Week," June 6, 2011, http://www.newsmax.com/Newsfront/ALLTOP-BDA-BNALL-BNSTAFF/2011/06/06/id/398982

13. Aaron Smith, CNNMoney, Joplin tornado damage could total $3 billion," http://money.cnn.com/2011/05/24/news/economy/tornado_joplin/index.htm

14. Laura Gottesdiener, *Huffington Post*, Natural Disasters Could Cost Tens of Billions in Economic Losses," http://www.huffingtonpost.com/2011/05/19/disasters-economic-losses_n_864449.html

15. Noah Buhavar, Bloomberg, "Joplin Leads Storms The May Cost $7 Billion in One Week," http://www.bloomberg.com/news/2011-06-06/joplin-tornado-leads-storms-that-may-cost-insurers-7-billion-in-one-week.html

CHAPTER TWELVE

1. Wikipedia, "First World War Casualties," http://en.wikipedia.org/wiki/World_War_I_casualties

2. Wikipedia, "Second World War Casualties," http://en.wikipedia.org/wiki/World_War_II_casualties

3. Rev. Bill Lee-Warner, "Is the reference in Daniel 8 to 2300 days a prophecy of Antiochus Epiphanes or Antichrist?" Sola Scriptura, http://www.solagroup.org/articles/faqs/faq_0017.html

CHAPTER THIRTEEN

1. Robert Young Pelton, *The World's Most Dangerous Places*, 4th ed. (New York: Times Books/Henry Holt and Company, 2004), p. 70.

2. Paul L. Williams, *The Al Qaeda Connection*, (New York: Prometheus Books), p. 83.

3. Ibid

4. Scott Parish & John Lepingwell, NTI Research Library, "Russia: Are Suitcase Nukes on the Loose? The story Behind the Controversy" November 1997, http://www.nti.org/db/nisprofs/over/lebedst.htm

5. Ibid

6. "The Perfect Terrorists Weapon," interview with Gen. Alexander Lebed, *60 Minutes*, CBS News, September 7, 1997

7. Ibid

8. *The Sunday Times*, September 20, 2009, "Investigation: Nuclear scandal – Dr Abdul Qadeer Khan, Simon Henderson, 4-5-2011, http://www.timesonline.co.uk/tol/news/world/asia/article6839044.ece

9. Ibid

10. Ibid

11. Tim Burger & Tim McGirk, "Al-Qaeda's Nuclear Contact?" *Time* May 19, 2003, http://www.time.com/time/printout/0,8816,1004867,00.html

12. Paul L. Williams, *The Al Qaeda Connection*, (New York: Prometheus Books), p. 113 & 197

13. Paul L. Williams, *The Al Qaeda Connection*, (New York: Prometheus Books), p. 192.

14. James Gordon Meek, *Daily News Washington Bureau*, "Former VP Dick Cheney warns of nuclear attack on United States under President Obama," February 4, 2009

15. "Ashcroft: Nuclear Bombs Biggest Threat in Terror War," *Columbia Daily Tribune*, January 28, 2005

16. Anton La Guardia, *The Telegraph*, "Divine mission driving Iran's new leader" January 14, 2006 http://www.telegraph.co.uk/news/worldnews/middleeast/iran/1507818/Divine-mission-driving-Irans-new-leader.html

17. Ibid

18. David Albright & Corey Hinderstein, The Center for Strategic and International Studies and the Massachusetts Institute of Technology, Unraveling the A Q Khan and future Proliferation Networks" Spring 2005, pp. 111-128

19. Ibid

20. Lewis Smith, *The Times*, "Seizures of Radioactive materials fuel 'dirty bomb' fears," October 6, 2006, http://www.timesonline.co.uk/tol/news/uk/crime/article663245.ece

21. Daniel Benjamin and Steven Simon, *The Age of Sacred Terror*, pp. 203-204

22. Robert Anson, "*The Journalist and the Terrorists*," Vanity Fair

23. Ibid

24. David Albright and Holly Higgings, How Much Nuclear Assistance to Al Qaeda?" Institute for Science and International Security, August 30, 2002 http://www.exportcontrols.org/pakscientists.html

25. Lewis Smith, *The Times*, "Seizures of Radioactive materials fuel 'dirty bomb' fears," October 6, 2006, http://www.timesonline.co.uk/tol/news/uk/ crime/article663245.ece

26. Paul L. Williams, *The Al Qaeda Connection*, (New York: Prometheus Books), p. 86.

27. Paul L. Williams, *The Al Qaeda Connection*, (New York: Prometheus Books), p. 77.

28. Frontline, "Osama bin Laden v. the U.S. Edicts and Statements," Accesses 4-2-20011, http://www.pbs.org/wgbh/pages/frontline/shows/binladen/ who/edits.html

29. Ibid

30. Ibid

31. Ibid

32. Ibid

33. Wm. Robert Johnson, Osama bin Laden and nuclear weapons, updated 9-22-202, http://www.johnsonsarchive.net/nuclear/osamanuk.html

34. Ibid

35. Ibid

36. Sarah Estabrooks, *The Ploughshares Monitor*, "Nuclear Terrorism," December 2001, Volume 22, No. 4 http://www.ploughshares.ca/libraries/ monitor/mond01b.html

37. Michael Evans, *The Sunday Times*, "Hillary Clinton fears al-Qaeda is obtaining nuclear weapons material," April 12, 2012 http://www. timesonline.co.uk/tol/news/world/us_and_americas/article7094876.ece

CHAPTER FOURTEEN

1. R. Brouwer, Major Battles, 2001, http://home.versatel.nl/rene.brouwer/majorbattles.htm

2. Philip Gibbs, *Now it can be told*, Garden City Publishing Co., 1920 pp. 6

3. Wikipedia, World War I, accessed 05/16/2011, http://en.wikipedia.org/wiki/World_War_I

4. Graham Allison, *Technology Review*, Massachusetts Institute of Technology, "Nuclear Deterrence in the Age of Nuclear Terrorism"

5. Ibid

6. Katie Frost, "Nuclear Terrorism: Are You Prepared?" Harvard Kennedy School Review: 2011 Edition, http://isites.harvard.edu/icb/icb.do?keyword=k74756&pageid=icb.page414662

7. Graham Allison, Technology Review, Massachusetts Institute of Technology, "Nuclear Deterrence in the Age of Nuclear Terrorism"

8. Ibid

9. Natural Resources Defense Council, "The ABC News Nuclear Smuggling Experiment : The Sequel" http://www.nrdc.org/nuclear/furanium.asp

10. Ibid

11. Weopine.com, "Terrorists Captured Entering US Through Mexico" May 21, 2010 http://weopine.com/index.php/terrorists-captured-entering-us-through

12. Ibid

13. *WSBTV.com*, "Terrorists Threat On Border With Mexico," May 3, 2010, http://www.wsbtv.com/print/23434381/detail.html

14. *Free Republic*, "Channel 2 Uncovers Proof Terrorists Crossed Mexican Border," November 10, 2010, http://www.freerepublic.com/focus/f-news/2620576/posts

15. Marc Schenker, *Examiner.com*, "Hezbollah terrorists entering the US through Mexican border; Obama ignors evidence," November 29, 2010,

http://www.examiner.com/american-politics-in-vancouver/hezbollah-
terrorists-entering-us-through-mexican-border-obama-ignores-evidence

16. Deroy Murdock, *Hacer Weekly News Report USA*, "U.S.-Mexican border
    is terrorists' moving sidewalk," June 24, 2010, http://www.hacer.org/
    usa/?p=424

17. House Committee on Homeland Security, "A Line in the Sand:
    Confronting the Threat at the Southwest Border,"

18. Newsmax, "Lieberman: Canadian Border Vulnerable to Terrorists,"
    February 1, 2011, http://www.newsmax.com/PrintTemplate.
    aspx?nodeid=384672

CHAPTER FIFTEEN

1. John F. Kennedy Presidential Library and Museum, Cuban Missile Crisis,"
   http://www.jfklibrary.org/JFK/JFK-in-History/Cuban-Missile-Crisis.
   aspx?view=print

2. Roger Hedgecock, WorldnetDaily, "Chinese ready to kill U.S.
   Navy carriers?" August 9, 2010, http://www.wnd.com/index.
   php?pageId=189193

3. *The Wall Street Journal*, "Obama's Missile Offense," September 18, 2009,
   http://online.wsj.com/article/SB10001424052970204518504574418563
   346840666.html

4. William Broad, *The New York Times*, "U.S. Rethinks Strategy for
   the Unthinkable," December 15, 2010, http://www.nytimes.
   com/2010/12/16/science/16terror.html?_r=1

5. Ibid

6. Michael Evans, *The Sunday Times*, "Hillary Clinton fears al-Qaeda
   is obtaining nuclear weapons material," April 12, 2010, http://www.
   timesonline.co.uk/tol/news/world/us_and_americas/article7094876.ece

7. *Free Republic*, "Al-Qaeda on brink of using nuclear bomb," February 1,
   2011, http://www.freerepublic.com/focus/f-news/2667102/posts

8. Anthony Martin, *Conservative Examiner*, "Wikileaks documents show al-Qaeda has nuclear bomb," February 2, 2011, http://www.examiner.com/conservative-in-national/wikileaks-documents-show-al-qaeda-has-nuclear-bomb

9. Associated Press, Fox Nation, "Wikileaks: Al-Qaeda on Brink of Using Nuclear Bomb," http://nation.foxnews.com/dirty-bomb/2011/02/01/wikileaks-al-qaida-brink-using-nuclear-bomb

10. Ibid

11. Graham Allison, *Technology Review*, Massachusetts Institute of Technology, "Nuclear Deterrence in the Age of Nuclear Terrorism"

12. Ibid

13. Oliver Burkeman, *The Guardian*, "How two students build an A-bomb," June 23, 2003, http://www.guardian.co.uk/world/2003/jun/24/use.science/print

14. Paul L. Williams, *The Al Qaeda Connection*, (New York: Prometheus Books), p. 96-98

15. Richard Sale, United Press International, "U.S. Investigating Whether Nukes In Country," Washington, December 20, 2001

16. Paul L. Williams, *The Al Qaeda Connection*, (New York: Prometheus Books), p. 96-98

17. Richard Sale, United Press International, "U.S. Investigating Whether Nukes In Country," Washington, December 20, 2001

18. Paul L. Williams, *The Al Qaeda Connection*, (New York: Prometheus Books), p. 96-98

19. Richard Sale, United Press International, "U.S. Investigating Whether Nukes In Country," Washington, December 20, 2001

20. Paul L. Williams, *The Al Qaeda Connection*, (New York: Prometheus Books), p. 96-98

21. Richard Sale, United Press International, "U.S. Investigating Whether Nukes In Country," Washington, December 20, 2001

22. Paul L. Williams, *The Al Qaeda Connection*, (New York: Prometheus Books), p. 96-98

23. Richard Sale, United Press International, "U.S. Investigating Whether Nukes In Country," Washington, December 20, 2001

24. Riyad 'Alam-al-Din, Al-Watan al-;Arabi, Moscow, November 13, 1998, http://nucleararchive.org/News/WatanAlArabi.html

25. Al Lewis, *Denver Post*, "Tancredo hit by hedge fund fallout," http://www.denverpost.com/business/ci_11619072

26. World Net Daily, "Why the U.S. has been terror-free since 9-11," January 7, 2005, http://www.wnd.com/news/article.asp?ARTICLE_ID=42272

27. David Sanger & Peter Baker, *The New York Times*, "Obama Limits When U.S. Would Use Nuclear Weapons," April 5, 2010, http://www.nytimes.com/2010/04/06/world/06arms.html?pagewanted=1

28. Elbridge Colby, *Weekly Standard*, "The New Deterrence," http://www.weeklystandard.com/Content/Public/Articles/000/000/014/959tnykn.asp

29. Ken Dilanian, *Los Angeles Times*, "CIA has slashed its terrorism interrogation role," http://articles.latimes.com/print/2011/apr/10/world/la-fg-cia-interrogation-20110411

CPSIA information can be obtained at www.ICGtesting.com
Printed in the USA
LVOW060311240113

316915LV00001BC/1/P

9 780615 526560